Power Up

Power Up

How to Improve Innovation and Productivity

Christine Wing Kit Yip

Published by C Why International Ltd.

First published in 2022 in Auckland, New Zealand

www.cwhy.co.nz

Auckland, New Zealand

Edited by Jenny Magee

Designed and typeset in Australia by BookPOD

Printed by Print House Ltd

ISBN: 978-0-473-61114-9 (paperback)

ISBN: 978-0-473-61116-3 (e-book)

Contents

Dedication and Acknowledgement

I dedicate this book to all my family, including my family from Hong Kong, my Kiwi host family, the Blofields from Reporoa, and the extended Ogilvie whānau in New Zealand. Without you all, I would not have become the person I am today. I am truly grateful for your love and support over the years. A special thanks to my other half, Glen Ogilvie, who is my rock, mirror and best friend as we share our interests in technologies and business.

To my friends and colleagues in professional communities in New Zealand and across many time zones, I value you all. Every workplace and community I have worked in is unique and holds a special place in my heart. I thank you for the time and experiences we've had together. Those experiences have enriched me and shaped the knowledge I present here.

A special thanks to Matt Church, Christina Guidotti, Linda Hutchings, Peter Cook, Col Fink and Lisa O'Neill for your mentoring, advice, and inspiration as role models showing the path of possibility.

Thank you to Joannah Bernard, Shane Williams, Bob Ratnarajah, Kirsten Peterson, Alan Hesketh, Joanne Flinn, Isabella Allan, Lisa Gerber, Jade Lee, Colleen Creighton and many others for your encouragement, peer support and time to bounce around book ideas. You are all inspiring, and I am grateful for the friendships we've developed.

Introduction

The global manufacturing and logistics industry is undergoing substantial challenges. Having been part of the sector for more than a decade, I have a passion for helping my fellow leaders to navigate these challenging times.

The sector has gone through several change cycles since the beginning of the industrial revolution. We are now seeing a further challenging time, and emerging leaders must be equipped to lead in the digital era.

We cannot avoid disruptions, but we can always learn from the past. The rapid change caused by the pandemic and acceleration of technologies is not going away any time soon. Consolidating and leveraging past wisdom for practical use will be vital in creating a thriving future.

Power Up distils my experience and observations in designing and implementing enterprise-wide improvement initiatives. As a Lean Six Sigma and Scrum Agile practitioner, I have used both methodologies extensively in my career. Six Sigma began as an engineering method to deliver quality results. The evolution of Six Sigma with Lean manufacturing has emerged to meet today's challenges. This book is based upon the four voices that are key to business improvement in the Lean Six Sigma methodologies (Sye, 2009; Kubiak & Benbow, 2016). My investigation concludes that these four voices stand the test of time and are crucial in the digital era.

Organisational process maturity is essential in designing and implementing sustainable improvement outcomes across the enterprise. My contribution is to share practical leverage experiences that you can apply in the forthcoming digital industrial revolution.

I am aware that professional development for manufacturing and transport teams is often a luxury, despite people working tirelessly to create our essential household supplies and keep the world moving. Since the pandemic, we've even elevated them with special titles as essential services workers. I believe there is an uneven distribution of knowledge in the sector. I sincerely hope the book will support the sector to embrace the opportunities to take operations to the next level and support growth in the digital era.

Though the book focuses on the manufacturing and logistics sectors, the lesson learnt are applicable to other sectors sharing similar characteristics.

Constraints and disruption

Manufacturing and logistics companies are in a unique position because they make and deliver actual goods, which means there are heavy financial constraints of factories, equipment, fleet, and material supplies. Their context is in complete contrast to web-based services or mobile apps created out of nothing and scaled at speed.

Another constraint is compliance with standards. Most companies must meet at least a handful of international or local legislation and quality standards. There is no such thing as a blank canvas here; they must create and deliver within defined boundaries of red tape. The sector is heavily reliant on people getting things done. With financial pressure to maintain physical assets and manage compliance risks, there is little room to explore how technologies and better systems can advance and ensure a sustainable future for the business.

Emerging trends such as driverless cars and smart roading infrastructure, the development of intelligent transport systems and smart cities will radically change the way people and goods move around the globe in the next decade or so.

That puts the sector in a relatively dangerous position as new technologies enable the emergence of ideas and business models. For example, the sharing economy has seen private vehicles turn into a delivery fleet and individual homes become tourist accommodations. Owning, leasing, and maintaining traditional infrastructure no longer offers a strong competitive advantage.

Enterprises have always acted like elephants, and now they are being overtaken by mice.

We may not yet know what further technology disruption looks like. However, we already recognise that the sector is struggling to gain higher margins. The supply chain is being disrupted, legacy systems are failing, there is constant firefighting and a distinct lack of investment in the people who make it all happen.

When the sector is too busy focusing on internal struggles, dismissing the external collective changes heading fast towards us is easy. Noisy internal battles overshadow the inner voices that want a more empowered future. How can the sector withstand the storm of disruptions and come out stronger on the other side – without a clear guiding voice?

Why this book?

My experience suggests there is an urgency to speed up the process to grow people and transform businesses to weather future disruption. I am confident that, individually, organisations hold the key to business advancement amid a disruptive world. It is a matter of unlocking the right doors – one at a time.

> The three major causes of headaches and overwork for executives are siloed thinking, legacy systems, and disengaged teams.

This book provides a fresh perspective for executives with practical tips to improve productivity and bottom-line revenue while working on future innovation.

The three major causes of headaches and overwork for executives are siloed thinking, legacy systems, and disengaged teams. Despite the immediate challenges of the disruptive business environment, there is pressure on senior executives to drive the organisation's vision and long-term business sustainability. Process variations lead to wasted effort, extra stress and a lack of clarity. The stakes are high, and few management resources address the problems faced by the sector.

This book offers pointers for improving performance and innovation based on recent sector experience. Executives can use the book to work on the business rather than in it, creating space to connect business situations with practical solutions.

CHRISTINE W.K. YIP

For emerging operational leaders, this book can fast-track your career to senior leadership by gaining a clear understanding of different aspects of the business and tapping into others' successes and failures. The practical steps to working with various business functions provide a glimpse into life in an executive leadership position.

I have seen the frustration of frontline and mid-level operational leaders who aspire to step into senior leadership roles. It is difficult to find management resources that solve their specific day-to-day issues, and their seniors often suggest that trial and error is the only way to learn. They have to take matters into their own hands to build credibility and a reputation for good performance to move up the ladder.

If there is good internal mentoring support, emerging leaders will strive, but it is not always available. Those bright, young leaders are seeing fewer senior roles available or the roles are taken by others with a stronger reputation for leadership. They have no way to build experience without years under their belts.

Unlike other sectors where young people with creative ideas can make a future of their own, emerging leaders work tirelessly to support their organisations without the reward of a leadership pathway. There is a strong temptation for them to move to more lucrative sectors.

The inability of the industry to retain the best and the brightest means fewer growth opportunities, which is reflected in the current shortage of young talent in leadership positions. It was an industry-wide issue before the pandemic, and the talent gap will continue to widen in the future.

How to use this book

Executives of the future need to build strategic ability to oversee every aspect of the business, including understanding the potential and challenges of digital technologies. Those who have already mastered a single business area, such as finance, sales, or human resources, can use this book for professional and organisational development.

Those from other sectors who have come into new leadership roles in manufacturing and logistics can absorb the stories throughout the book to create their own recipe for success.

Power Up Model

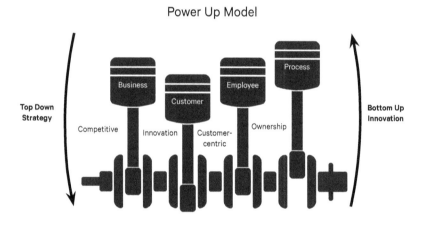

Figure 1: Bottom Up Innovation

The **Power Up model** describes the four voices as the cylinders of an engine necessary to drive the business forward. The cylinders are responsible for the compression process for the vehicle to move and function. The four cylinders (or voices) are Business, the Customer, the Employee and Process.

The engine is the key to the performance of the vehicle. Similarly, sustainable business performance takes all four voices to drive progress and continuous momentum.

The cylinders take turns to mix air and fuel to create consistent energy to move the wheels. The compression process in a combustion engine runs quietly and smoothly – humming when it goes well.

When issues cause the cylinders to have no compression, the car will not start. When some cylinders stop working, the driver might experience a misfire starting the engine or poor vehicle performance when accelerating.

My observation is that the Voice of Business and the Voice of the Customer are the cylinders that lead organisations through performance and financial data. While they fulfil a particular function in leading the business towards a prosperous vision, the articulation and execution require sustainable momentum from the rest.

> Powering up business performance is more than having a well-run engine. Good alignment of the body parts is a must. When the processes connecting the various functions are aligned, the vision and the strategy are implemented to achieve the desired outcomes.

Powering up business performance is more than having a well-run engine. Good alignment of the body parts is a must. When the processes connecting the various functions are aligned, the vision and the strategy are implemented to achieve the desired outcomes. Manoeuvring safely across tricky terrain requires a vehicle that is running well, with effective steering, aligned wheels and good tyres.

> With reduced barriers to implementing technology, the key now is the ability to align them with the business functions and processes to ensure the improvement delivers value to the organisation and return on investment.

Businesses that own assets such as fleet and plant cannot easily move from their current operational infrastructure, though they can improve their ability to survive and thrive in challenging conditions through improvement in innovation and productivity in people, process and technologies.

The good news is that new technology and innovation are increasingly available and affordable to logistics and manufacturing businesses. With reduced barriers to implementing technology, the key now is the ability to align them with the business functions and processes to ensure the improvement delivers value to the organisation and return on investment.

The book is arranged in four parts.

Part One is the Voice of Business. We discuss business data and how to discover meaningful insights for decision-making.

We'll explore the relationship between efficiency, profitability and technology innovation from a practical perspective.

Part Two is the Voice of the Customer. Here we look at how to listen better to the customers' needs as an integrated business, and the part technologies play in uncovering new insights and service delivery innovation.

In Part Three, the Voice of the Employee, we consider how the vision, strategy and business structure influence team behaviour and motivation, driving innovation with technology and business sustainability.

Part Four is the Voice of the Process, which examines how the enterprise processes can be designed to deliver strategic outcomes for the business with the alignment of new technology. We discuss the relationship between process maturity and the pathways to digitalise the operation processes.

Operational leaders are often time-poor, so relevant examples are easy to find, making it simple for your team to go through the various voices and apply the ideas and techniques.

I want this book to contribute to the sector as part of a more diverse and inclusive voice. Our environment is changing with more women and young people taking leadership roles, and I hope they benefit from the experiences and the shared learning within these pages.

PART ONE

THE VOICE OF BUSINESS

The joy of operating a business is the satisfaction of solving problems successfully. Since March 2020, the world has experienced dramatic disruption of our ways of living, working and doing business. Leaders need to evolve radically in response to the pandemic and its ongoing effect. There is a difference between choosing to survive or thrive in the future. Surviving businesses need to make a profit to stay afloat while thriving businesses meet the challenges head-on.

The Voice of Business brings clarity to performance with measurements and data. It's not just the voice of finance, even though money is a crucial measure. Instead, it is a channel to tune into the needs and opportunities of the business. This voice ensures financial sustainability and operational stability in the long run. As a growth indicator, it provides insights into whether the business vision has been achieved.

Profitability

Thriving in a changing environment

The cost of goods is increasing as the world faces global logistical challenges from the current pandemic and subsequent disruption to the supply chain.

We have been fortunate over the past decade. Improvements in global logistics brought just-in-time manufacturing, ensuring sufficient supplies of goods produced overseas at reasonable prices. Much of today's lifestyle is built on the convenience of buying cheaper goods from overseas directly through online shopping.

Many of us remember when goods and services were not readily available via our keyboards. My annual family visit to Asia was also a shopping trip to restock goods I could not access in New Zealand. Eventually, I've found local replacements to serve the same purpose, but that took a while. Things changed when I could order online and receive goods delivered directly to my home.

Similarly, businesses now face supply disruption and increasing operational costs on top of the effect of the pandemic. The price of shipping containers increased more than tenfold between 2020 and 2021, making international trade less profitable. Disrupted shipping costs have impacted internationally-traded components to finished products and the distribution of goods and services. The transportation sector is facing shortages of labour and energy, with the price of natural gas hiking more than 700 per cent between 2020 and 2021 (Cowen, 2021). Gone are the days when we could expect an order to turn up within the service target timeframe.

Sourcing locally is another challenge as many countries have slimmed down manufacturing in the past decade because of a lack of global competitive advantage. The uncertainty of immigration policies, border closures and travel restrictions have also affected labour costs in businesses that rely on skilled workers to pick up the seasonal workload and freight availability. Increases in material costs have massive repercussions for business profitability.

The pandemic climate and global political uncertainty has also seen rising compliance costs, with the need to provide staff with personal protective equipment, segregate people on-site as required, and additional labour costs involved in coordinating this work. Executives have not previously had to consider how much these extras eat into the minimal margins of their business.

Some businesses have seen revenue decline due to social distancing or lockdown impacting physical retail sales, less demand for luxurious consumer goods and potential reduction of disposable income across their customer segments.

For others, business is booming because of a sudden demand surge, but staff overheads, infrastructure, and compliance costs have also increased. In either case, the flow-on effect to vendors and supplier operations is enormous. It is a challenging and uncertain time for the manufacturing and logistics industry to survive and thrive.

I know it is a cliché, but every crisis brings opportunity. Most people don't want to hear how things can be better in happy times because life is already pretty good. In crisis mode, though, we have no choice except to face the hard truth. A crisis gives us the courage to reset the way forward. It is a much-needed reality check for some to consider which new problems need resolving in the market and the drivers impacting profitability in the business.

> A crisis gives us the courage to reset the way forward.

If the crisis brings the opportunity for growth, we must ask what kind of growth we are aiming to achieve? There are typically three types of business growth: linear, incremental and rock star.

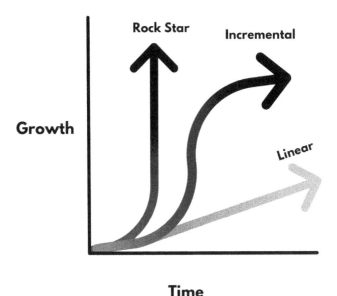

Figure 2: The three growth paths

The three growth paths

Linear growth happens in small, exact quantities in a set period. It's like jogging at a consistent pace. While some people can manage a brisk pace of four minutes per kilometre, others might choose a more leisurely pace. Both will finish at their own speed.

Incremental growth is similar in that it happens through micro-improvements over a long period. Yet, this is the path of risk aversion and security to ensure the business sticks to what is working well. Innovation is localised without substantially changing how things are done due to red tape, policy and a collective mindset for safety.

To reduce risk, larger enterprises tend to follow the same set of best practices without assessing real needs or adding restrictions to the standard frameworks. Financial and management best practices are great frameworks until they become part of the red tape problem.

The *S-shaped sigmoid* growth curve sees results building up slowly in the beginning and gaining momentum into rapid growth. It takes time to develop new ways and gain momentum, at which point the accumulated effort accelerates growth quickly. Breakthrough is likely to accompany problem-solving and breaking the status quo, leading to rapid growth.

Yeast is a good example of S-shaped growth when it has the resources (sugar) and environment (warmth) to grow rapidly, causing the bread dough to rise. When the sugar is used up, the yeast stops growing, and the dough stops rising. It becomes the new status quo.

Rock Star growth is the J-shape exponential curve, where little time is needed to gain rapid momentum. We know that bacteria grow exponentially because their DNA is designed to do so unless a force or disruption halts the process. Businesses can reinvent their DNA to be completely different from the past. Such change and transformation can pose significant risks even though it can be the fastest way to grow.

For organisations, the too-hard basket might be a breeding ground for new DNA that enables the organisation to evolve. Leaders need time and space to reflect with their teams and discover the ongoing issues that have been difficult to resolve.

New solutions are possible with a fresh perspective, a different operating environment and new technology.

The business growth cycle

There are six stages in the business growth cycle. Ideating, Developing, Market-testing, Scaling up, Sustaining and Regenerating.

Identifying which stage they are at helps businesses understand the Voice of Business and determine the best plan of attack.

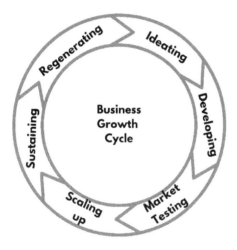

Figure 3: The business growth cycle

Most sizeable traditional manufacturing and logistics businesses are likely to be at the sustaining or regenerating stage. They have championed incremental continuous improvement in the past, but rapid and ad hoc rearrangement of the operation suspends improvement efforts. Abandoning continuous improvement principles will see them struggle when the market returns with significant demand for their services. On the other hand, innovative new businesses that are strong on iterating with improvements can rapidly scale up with new technologies, achieving exponential rock star growth.

Innovative businesses can move rapidly from ideating to scaling-up and disrupt the market status quo with the advantage of new technologies, a different business model, and minimal historical baggage. Traditional manufacturers and transportation suppliers need to look at ways to regenerate the business quickly.

Accelerated digital investment

The pandemic has been a driving force to switch on digital capabilities. Businesses are speeding up their investment in acquiring and implementing new technologies in response to the need to work remotely and do business online.

Significant investment in technology and infrastructure can reduce business profitability in the interim and impact the shareholders' perception of the board and executive performance. Most shareholders focus on consistent year-on-year returns on investment in their shares, and lower profitability will affect the dividends. There is also too little reassurance that the technology investment will deliver the promised return on investment for some.

It has always been hard to justify technology investment for a low margin, high infrastructure overhead business with largely manual procedures. That includes the manufacturing, transportation and logistics industries. Lack of investment means some may not have been investing and maintaining their digital systems as they should have been. The chances are they chose, instead, to invest in ad hoc solutions in silos to meet the needs. There is little overall understanding of future technology requirements.

The decision to withhold much-needed technology investment resulted in some businesses falling into technology debt, meaning they lag behind reasonable technology standards. Technology debt is usually coupled with a lack of internal people capability in the same space. The team finds ways to work around poor standards of systems and technologies, but the business suffers low productivity and efficiency.

The hard truth is that no one can do a good job without sufficient systems and tools. If the business has suffered from this issue, it is time to map out ways to get out of debt, regardless of whether it is related to technology or capability. The incremental way is by getting the basics right and investing in small steps toward building future prosperity. Greater growth, however, requires new investment. Radically reviewing the business and technology strategy in light of future markets and investment in the necessary infrastructure will enable growth into a new era.

Uncover true performance

To drive growth, we must know the current baseline. The Profit and Loss statement (P&L) is the most common reporting tool for understanding business health. It realistically captures dollar transactions and amounts, so it is essentially a financial performance measurement tool. The way the reporting structure is built can also indicate which parts of the business are ripe for growth.

Although the P&L is rich in data and logic, it may not be easy to analyse unless you understand the history of the business. Historical decisions and underlying rules impact the equation and affect the numbers represented. For an organisation with a rich history, it can mean that the Profit and Loss structure needs to be modified periodically, given changes to functional departments. The changes almost certainly mean turnover of people and lost internal knowledge. Without continuity of transactions and an understanding of the history of the business, it can be extremely difficult to understand the actual performance of the business functions over time.

One hidden trap in analysing the Profit and Loss is how operational transactions are handled. A lag in data input or incomplete data entry due to mishandling can affect the end of the month reporting and impact the overall financial performance. For team leaders and department heads who are new to the details in operations, it can be mistaken as a complete list of transactions for month-end data submission. With good teamwork between the financial and operations departments, the transactions impacted are identified and can be manually adjusted to reflect the reality and minimise the discrepancy.

A useful watchpoint is that the need for manual adjustments likely means more issues to resolve in the operational process. The financial data submission is a clean-cut date and time, and operational activities must be completed before the deadline. It should be the fundamental principle for teams, and we must ask questions about any delay or lack of transaction data for reporting. It may be a simple educational exercise to reiterate the deadline, but asking the team for evidence of what prevented them from meeting expectations helps identify upstream issues.

For executives and teams taking over a new function, it can be a lengthy process to find out the history and stories of the business that impact ongoing, unresolved performance issues. People's memories are not always reliable. With a keen eye for detail, executives can understand the true performance of the operational process between the lines of dollar amounts in the Profit and Loss statement.

The financial statement has become the go-to place to understand the status of a business because of the lack of data and transparency of operational performance. Understanding actual performance is the groundwork for preparing and uncovering potential commercial innovations.

> Understanding actual performance is the groundwork for preparing and uncovering potential commercial innovations.

Depending on the data maturity, symptoms of operational data availability in operations can be summarised as follows:

➜ Manual processes that generate no quantitative data recorded in any format.

➦ Manual processes with manual data entry by the team. (Although this offers no guarantee that the data was captured and entered correctly.)

➦ Mechanical and manual processes, with no data captured. This is related to production, where people handle the materials and use machines to produce the goods.

➦ Hybrid digital mechanical processes with data availability issues. Despite having some digital mechanism in place, the data is captured but not available for analysing or reporting.

➦ Fully digitalised processes with limited data accessibility. The data is captured, but a lack of access is a barrier to leveraging available data.

Digital systems do not guarantee data accessibility and performance transparency, although the worst-case scenario has absolutely no operational data due to the way the business is set up. In this case, the solution is reverse problem-solving, which means working back from the Profit and Loss statement to find clues of the performance opportunities.

More granular operational data can take away the guesswork from analysing the Profit and Loss, enabling stronger working relationships across functions and much-needed insights into the core business. The data can show where improvement or innovation is needed internally or externally.

The absence of reliable operational data is a challenge in the manufacturing and transport sectors. The good news is that affordable technologies now make it possible to gather data that was previously impossible to reliably record manually.

Automated data collection technologies can be built into the workflow to collect data at set times or triggers using wirelessly connected measurement hardware. These then present the data in an automated dashboard for analysis. The availability of real-time data insights and mobile technology can reveal gaps in the current business model and lead to exploring new business opportunities.

Sense and sensibility with technologies

Despite the vision of growth and a more connected future business, some traditional manufacturing and logistics businesses experience a lack of momentum in building digital capability and systems. While the board pushes for a more digitalised business, middle layer managers fail to see how it can benefit their day-to-day operational performance. It doesn't help that expensive digital systems often fail to deliver expected benefits, let alone the return on investment stated.

> Scope creep is common in technology investment.

The immediate need to maintain a healthy level of profitability is key as it ties into the operational performance structure for the people on the receiving end. For many operational leaders, fear of the unknown comes with the risk of destabilising performance and potentially losing personal power and authority. This causes change resistance and low uptake of technologies, delaying implementation and incurring additional costs. There needs to be operational buy-in through involvement and understanding of the technologies and future processes before starting the change programme. That involvement can be a physical visit to the shop floor to understand the current way of working, engaging with dialogue, and warming up the team with the possibility of implementing tools to improve their working conditions. The key here is building the people-to-people connection and engaging them in a vision of the future that they are a part of.

Scope creep is common in technology investment. Scope is the area of work that a project is bound to deliver to meet business requirements. The problem is when too many ideas and needs are identified, and the scope of work grows unexpectedly. The broader the scope of work, the more expensive it is for software development. The upfront capital investment required to develop customised technology and software is a significant roadblock for businesses.

Large organisations tend to acquire off-the-shelf packaged software solutions and customise them for localised functionality. This happens even though these solutions can provide the necessary business functionality. Unless the scope and functionality are carefully considered and prioritised, the development cost increases unnecessarily. The ongoing maintenance goes up, diminishing any future possibility of standard system updates from the original software developing company.

Excessive modifications of off-the-shelf enterprise software become yet another legacy system. Organisations struggle to maintain these systems despite using some big-name providers. Once you add staff turnover, and dated hardware and software, it is not difficult to understand why some of the enormous investments don't always bring a good return.

The lack of a standardised process when identifying user requirements can also be the reason for scope creep in technology investment. Although the team delivers certain business activities manually, they don't follow a standardised way of working. It becomes more complex when we add different geographical locations and countries to the mix. For example, how many ways can you cook an egg? That simple question reminds us how a single small item can turn into thousands of different outcomes.

Imagine you consult users across the globe on their method of cooking an egg and develop one technological solution to deliver results that cater for all their differences. It is almost impossible to build because of the complexity of technologies involved and the excessive price tag that comes with it. Without being justified and prioritised, the variation of the preferences and the process will become overwhelming and needlessly extend the scope of the investment with additional cost.

Advocating for digital infrastructure change can be a career breaker. Unless delivered to expectations, digital infrastructure implementation can become a political time bomb for leaders advocating for the investment. It is easier to put it in the too-hard basket or simply implement fragmented technologies as the opportunity arises, even though a lack of consistent digital infrastructure can hold the business back and lead to missed opportunities.

Leaders need to be mindful of the challenges and identify practical steps to navigate the political landscape while balancing the opportunity to drive the business forward.

A scope of work must be developed and aligned tightly with the vision statement. It would be reasonable to assess the risks involved with the changes, ensuring a good level of digital leadership with technical understanding as part of the governance process. The technology design and development are measured with return on investment (RoI) and end-user feedback. Communication with internal and external communities will ensure immediate feedback on the deliverables and safeguard the value provided by the technology. Transparency of progress, based on real-time project data, helps the governance team understand whether any issues or resistance are delaying the momentum of the new digital infrastructure. Ensuring all parties involved, including system vendors, business line leaders and customers, align in the shared ideal vision helps drive the vision forward.

Growth with innovation

A good leader needs to understand how to create opportunities to increase business profitability. Loosely speaking, there are two ways to do this organically without completely changing the business model or reinventing the wheel. These are increasing revenue or reducing expenses. Simple.

Well, not exactly. Improving revenue often requires investment in new products or sales activities. Even if we are willing to get started, the new options can take time to come to fruition in a large business.

Reducing expenses needs to happen with consideration of the real needs of the operation. It cannot be an exercise of numbers on paper. Without business understanding, it can disrupt the core business and cost extra in managing poor-quality outcomes.

We can also look at it as a balance of both, creating additional value for the end-users while reducing expenditure. How can you know if the business is heading in the right direction for better profit? There are five steps to creating rock star growth:

Inspection

➜ What is the future vision?

➜ Which are the business activities to look at?

➜ Are they aligned with the future vision?

Assess

➜ How do you assess the commercial value of the activities?

➜ What new value is on offer?

➜ Can the value be quantified in the cost and pricing?

Formulate

➜ What is the new process?

➜ Is there transparency of the true cost of service?

➜ Who needs to be on board internally?

Decide

➜ Which features are to stay?

➜ How does your market perceive the ideas?

➤ Is it an improvement of a current service, an add-on or a new offering?

Evolve

➤ How will you trial and validate the innovation?

➤ How can you measure emerging market needs?

➤ What is the success criteria?

In an uncertain environment, anchoring the activities with a purpose can help businesses clarify the added value, streamlining actions to innovation and, therefore, profitability. It can be the quickest way to drive growth by creating new revenue and reducing the cost of service. We will further explore what and how to do this in the coming chapters.

Case study: SkyRocket

SkyRocket specialises in manufacturing natural supplements from sheep's milk, which its global consumers know as unique products for improving bone health in older people. Since its launch in 2001, the supplements have been particularly popular with the Asian market. Over time, the company grew with a $389.7 million profit per annum over FY2018/2019. Seeing the increasing demand from the off-shore markets, SkyRocket was on track to expand with a new investment in a processing facility and a strategy to diversify the product range to improve long-term market sustainability.

With the disruption of the pandemic in 2020 and the subsequent supply chain delay, SkyRocket was hit hard by a sudden drop in demand and sluggish export sales in the following year. Their annual profit dropped 80 per cent to $90 million per annum in FY2020/2021. Rapid rising global dairy trade prices, foreign exchange, and a changing product mix created volatility and limited the return on investment in the following year. That changed the company's outlook as well as its strategic priority. It needed to focus on survival and holding on until the export market picked up.

The executive team had to make some hard decisions and do whatever was practicable to free up cash flow. Some big-ticket items on the Profit and Loss statement needed tackling to limit outgoing cash and help the company survive. These included immediate actions such as selling and releasing its new facility as an asset, reducing staff numbers by 20 per cent and reviewing the operational strategy.

The leadership team looked at the next most significant expenses and involved the team in reviewing potential wastage in operations and identifying possible solutions. The team learned the costs associated with materials used and labour costs in operations. They helped redistribute resources and staffing from the old operations model to a new model more aligned with the current business needs. As they were part of the process, they fully understood the change and advocated for the upcoming plan, leading others in the new direction.

With a new operational strategy, the team was tasked with a new purpose to support SkyRocket to recover financially through such a difficult time. The financial leadership responsibility was spread across the organisation, allowing the whole team to contribute to bottom-up innovation that could open up new revenue opportunities within their current resources.

The team came up with a new idea from their current product range to meet the local youth market. A new weekly innovation forum brought ideas for new revenue streams, and new products were created in small batches and tested with local partners as new sales channels. SkyRocket has now started to pick up revenue streams in the local market. Being highly resilient, SkyRocket will likely thrive with both local and off-shore markets resulting in a more sustainable and prosperous business outlook in the long term.

Operational performance indicators

Businesses rely on operations to create value-added services and products for customers. Operational resilience is even more significant in an uncertain environment as it is the core business of income generation and controlling expenditure.

Having financial information in the Profit and Loss statement is only a small part of understanding the performance of the operations. The greater understanding comes from five operational performance indicators in day-to-day management: health and safety, materials, labour, time and schedule, and compliance.

> Operational resilience is even more significant in an uncertain environment.

Operational performance indicators are the best way to understand the immediate customer demands and production and delivery needs. Setting up the measures with the right level of expectations and targets helps the team focus on their jobs and align the activities to the overall outcomes. The day-to-day insights can lead to unexpected innovation in ways of working and service offerings.

Health and safety

With its direct link to the health of employees and the organisation, this is a key priority. The most basic starting point of health and safety management is identifying risks, hazards, near misses, and incidents. By recognising safety risks early, we know that the number of hazards lessens, subsequently reducing near misses and incidents at workplaces.

It is a preventative approach with leading indicators that achieve ongoing education and build awareness of safety amongst the team. With greater understanding comes proactive preventive action. Most people have heard of the safety indicators mentioned above, though it would be wrong to assume they share the same understanding. It is important to flesh out the purpose of the health and safety programme. Engage the team on their needs and desires to better understand their version of workplace safety requirements. This helps make performance metrics more meaningful to those who use them as their daily guide.

Basic metrics can include the number of hazards identified and near misses and incidents reported daily. Keeping it simple helps the team understand the process of data gathering, getting used to the new concept of identifying and seeing the risks and hazards in their day-to-day work.

Learning and embedding this awareness can take time depending on the team's starting awareness and their sense of psychological safety at work. It is useful for senior management to deliberately build trusting relationships with the team as part of the work programme. Regular safety roadshows, a safety hall of fame, or simply an online Q&A forum can demonstrate commitment to safety and building trust. Sharing the importance of health and safety for business continuity with employee-focused exercises is crucial to gaining buy-in from the shop floor.

Day-to-day health and safety reporting should be a shared responsibility of the team and operation management. The team can suggest and immediately implement action upon identifying any safety issues, but the ultimate responsibility for ensuring corrective action lies with management. Some changes, such as handing over equipment on the ramp with external suppliers, are inter-departmental improvements and require management support. The assurance of management support is a crucial settling factor in building trust and the willingness to make positive changes in the workplace.

To analyse the data, look at the periodic intervals and compare numbers by the day. It sounds simple but is fundamental for a new team. Building a habit of understanding and explaining the daily numbers strengthens the team's awareness and develops their problem-solving abilities. Once they are familiar with the daily routine, try a more sophisticated analysis through health and safety incident systems to identify the different metrics reported. Seeing trends can bring them back to daily discussions to recognise the consistent issues and potentially reveal more insights into why specific hazards persist.

Another way to gain insights from the health and safety data is to relate it to other operational metrics. These might include the number of hours worked and the number of products created, to understand (on average) how many hazards, near misses, and incidents are related to the volume of products or services and the relationship between workload and safety. Equalising the numbers using a standardised formula such as the number of incidents per hundred work hours across various sites clarifies performance across multiple locations despite different shift lengths or work hours. There is a potential to analyse the frequency and time of day with the reported incidents in more granular detail.

Off-the-shelf health and safety incident systems are largely standardised based on compliance legislation requirements. Some systems are specifically designed to meet stricter requirements, such as the European Union or American legislation. That means that generic software can cater for most needs in most workplaces.

Teams can be deterred from engaging with safety initiatives and data gathering if management enforces the health and safety policy as a tick-box exercise. It can feel irrelevant and boring, knowing that nothing will change. With such history and lack of trust, the team can feel that health and safety are someone else's business, even when directly related to them.

Health and safety is a performance indicator that must be created jointly with the team for buy-in. For the safety programme to work in people's best interest, it cannot be done with hollow intention. The key success factor is allowing time for the team to learn and review their work environment. Consistency of management support, proactive listening, and actions in resolving any systemic issues on safety across the business create a healthy and trusting environment.

Materials

From printing paper to the diesel in the tank of the fleet, the true cost of materials can be complex and challenging to assess, so start with a helicopter view to thoroughly understand the cost of materials.

The journey of business activity is like walking from one end of a bridge to the other. Usually, people wander along looking at the scenery, but here you need to inspect the architecture and observe the materials holding up the platform. This level of awareness is essential. Business activity starts with service design and ends when the after-sales service is completed. Whether you can identify all the costs involved depends on where you look.

> The true cost of materials can be complex and challenging to assess.

Training your observation skills can take time – depending on your familiarity with the activity – and taking it to the next level can be a daily exercise involving several actions and materials at different times. Observe and identify the activities involved and materials usage along the way. Once familiar, you can go through a larger business end-to-end process with more comfort. It is like knowing how bridges connect to the wider city and impact traffic flow.

The concept of the end-to-end business process is an important part of the material cost indicator. Just like preparing a meal, the activity starts before the cooking. If the meal includes guests, then the invitation is the starting point. The work ends when the guests have left, and the dishes are done. It's the same in a business process. The starting point is an invitation to the customer to buy your product or service, and the end is when they have completed their experience.

Why do we take this full-spectrum approach to business processes for material cost? Because it is easy to simply identify a small area of work without realising the impact of upstream and downstream effects.

For a dinner party, groceries are only one of the material costs involved. Don't forget the candles on the dining table, power for the heat pump, and the extra load of dishes through the dishwasher. Usually, it would seem unnecessary to count those things as expenses for a dinner party. A business operation is different and requires training to observe the usage of materials.

Scaling up a cooking operation can mean purchasing simple ingredients such as salt, pepper, and dishwashing liquid in bulk quantities. The cost of those materials can have a major impact on the overall cost. If your team has trouble identifying ongoing material cost issues of the operation, then training them in observation will likely open their eyes to a greater awareness of the operations processes.

In a higher-level operational process, start by identifying the parties involved in managing the operational materials:

- customer
- sales
- procurement
- operations management
- supplier
- finance (optional)
- product development or quality team (optional).

Here is how we usually plan a walkthrough of the high-level business process.

It starts with conversations with the sales team to clarify the customer's expectations and service requirements. The team can offer an existing service or create a new commercial bespoke offering to suit the customer.

The sales department engages with operations management and procurement to define the specifications of the goods and services needed to produce and transport the finished goods and services. This is relative to the price and value customers expect to receive.

With the contractual commitment of customers who pay for an existing service, sales, procurement, and operations can generally decide on the additional goods and services that will deliver the outcomes and keep the financial team informed of these extra activities.

If upfront capital investment is involved in servicing the customer, the finance department needs to be part of the discussion early during the customer contractual negotiation. This especially applies to a bespoke product or service involving new machinery. Similarly, the product development team or quality team needs to be part of the early discussions with customers for a product that is radically different from current offerings. That will ensure the output complies with the quality standards and legal requirements where applicable.

Once the departments have reached an agreement, the procurement team purchases the goods and services, which are placed in storage until they are needed. The goods are scheduled to be transformed into products by the team, then the logistics process delivers the completed goods and services to the customers.

SIPOC analysis: Supplier, Inputs, Processes, Outputs and Customer

A walkthrough of a generic high-level business process is useful but can be confusing. That's because the personnel involved can overlap in multiple activities, and the activities happen concurrently. One way to obtain more clarity during the walkthrough is to use the following SIPOC analysis to divide the people and processes.

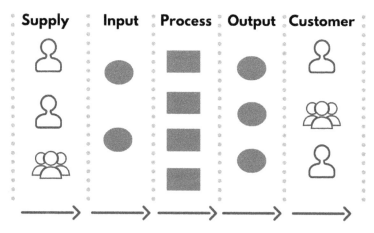

Figure 4: Visual SIPOC analysis

If we use a food delivery service as an example, then power for the vehicle is essential. Knowing the quantity and frequency of the power input, the distance and the average number of deliveries clarify the cost of the service.

SIPOC analysis for food delivery service

Supplier	Inputs	Process	Outputs	Customer
Car manufacturer Petrol / charging station Food outlet	Petrol/ battery level Location information Food order details Food to be delivered	Driving Food storage	Food moved from outlet to customer	Receiving food

The following are examples of high-level process analysis in manufacturing and transportation business activities. Using a visual method, the type of materials and the quantity supplied as input are crystal clear. The quantity of materials sold, ordered, and used is another way to measure the flow of materials and the performance of the process.

What is the process for manufacturing?

Supplier	Inputs	Process	Outputs	Customer
Provide raw materials to specifications	Raw materials	Transform materials to finished goods	Finished goods	Receive finished goods and needs met

What is the process for transportation?

Supplier	Inputs	Process	Outputs	Customer
Vehicles and materials supply	Transportation fleet Logistical details of what is transported, locations, pickup and dropoff times	Transporting materials or people	Arrival of materials or people at the destinations	Need to have people or products arriving at designated locations at specific times

When a box of stationery arrives by courier at the doorstep, most of us check that the goods match the order. Goods and products purchased need to be reconciled with the unit ordered and the number of units transported. At first glance, this is a straightforward activity, but it can take some training and coordinating effort in a busy warehouse that receives goods from multiple suppliers through a team of people. Receipting the wrong goods, lesser quantities, and poor quality can contribute to higher material costs. The transaction information across the suppliers, procurement team, and accounts payable team are clear and concise for analysis when it comes to an unexpected cost increase in materials.

The way materials are used also contributes to the cost. The risk here is when the material unit measurements and yields of the materials are not fully understood, and the usage method has not been agreed to or adhered to in the operational process. An easy example of this is the excessive use of detergent by whoever washes the dishes at home.

In production terms, if a food manufacturer expects to sell 100 sandwiches made with standard white bread, you can expect

100x2=200 slices of white bread, plus a minor variation to allow for unexpected errors.

However, the material cost changes if the customer's order changes from a standard to an artisan bread loaf. The supplier's material cost is based on an agreed specification of the number of slices per loaf. Monitoring the delivery consistency and the usage of the bread slices becomes crucial with a higher cost ingredient. That ensures that the materials purchased will produce the number of units customers expect to receive.

Transportation container units are also a significant pain point for manufacturers and logistics companies. If we expect to use ten container units to transport a certain quantity of goods (as per the agreement), it needs to be adhered to.

Exceeding the usage of materials and goods from the agreed amount can cause a flow-on impact on the rest of the operational processes and the financial performance. Shortage of materials causing unnecessary emergency procurement activities are costly to the business. The disruption of the material forecast and estimation based on the sales agreement and the overall operational requirements will add to rework to all parties involved and reduce productivity.

One way to have more transparency in transportation is through a cost attached per container unit usage as internal stock. It provides clarity in the movement of the unit in a distributed geographical network.

As seen in the examples above, the positive and negative variations of material cost in the financial transactions can represent the effectiveness of the operation process in materials control and usage. Given the significant cost attached to the material management space, there is room for a technology-driven innovative approach to managing material resources.

Labour

Despite having automation and machinery, manufacturing and logistics businesses are heavily dependent on people to create and deliver the products and services. The scalability and flexibility of the labour force ensure the operation is running as efficiently as possible in people resources. A survey conducted by US accounting firm Smith Schafer & Associates expected wages to account for 12.3 per cent of revenue in the manufacturing industry for 2021 (Smith Schafer, 2021). It is a significant percentage for a relatively small margin industry.

Wages alone do not reflect the actual cost of labour. Some of the non-wage components are:

- ➜ annual leave and statutory holidays
- ➜ superannuation
- ➜ social security or national insurance employer premiums
- ➜ medical insurance
- ➜ motor vehicles available for private use
- ➜ low-interest loans
- ➜ other non-taxable employee benefits.

The seasonal workload can impact labour demand and supply in the market. Think of a food manufacturer of Christmas hampers and a transport company. Operationally, both require qualified forklift operators and truck drivers to move goods across the site. While the transport company always needs forklift operators, their seasonal demand increases at Christmas. At the same time, other companies also compete for people with the same skillset because of seasonal demand. With a limited supply of qualified staff in the labour market, it can be difficult and costly to source extra staff during peak season.

Labour cost is not only a significant component of the cost of operation; you may have goods that must be produced and delivered, yet not enough hands on the floor to physically get the work done on time. If there is no mechanism to bring in flexible people resources, the level of stress and frustration can quickly escalate. If similar situations recur often, it will have a flow-on impact on the operational and financial performance of the business.

Forward workforce planning is essential in seeking the same skillsets in the market. Tactics such as hiring and training junior staff, providing a more competitive salary and flexibility in the roster schedule are standard practices to ensure sufficient staffing levels for the expected seasonal workload. To take it even further, technology automation that frees up labour hours can also be investigated.

Who is involved in managing the operational labour?

- ➔ Operations management
- ➔ Human Resources
- ➔ Finance

- ➜ Procurement (optional)
- ➜ External agency (optional)

There are different ways to set up an operational workforce with various contract types and skillsets. A large percentage of long-term contract or permanent staff is necessary for stability, availability, and a richer knowledge base. As the workload increases, knowledge and experience are needed to navigate complex schedules, work procedures and support on-the-job learning for temporary team members. If the operational tasks are relatively simple and repetitive, then temporary contracts are ideal for coping with the uncertain workload and ensuring the workforce is scalable.

Setting up a workforce is like mixing a cocktail. There are recipes available as guidance, but it's important to consider individual preferences and needs, so the cocktail is well received. Similarly, no two operations work in precisely the same way. A greater level of business understanding and engaging with the human resources team for longer-term planning should help navigate the industry's disruptions in the external environment.

Time and schedule

Every business has time constraints when it comes to performing operational tasks. Time is the essence of high performance in the manufacturing and logistics sector.

Time is a currency that we cannot scale up or down by changing the clock. It is not true that production goes faster with more people on the floor. The only way forward is to plan with a detailed understanding of the operational activities and buffers strategically placed in the schedule. It assures the schedule – even when operational activities may have taken longer than expected.

Delivery expectations are driven mainly by customers who have paid for a service or product. From that expectation, reverse problem-solving identifies the logistical constraints, the production time, and the initial setup time. An operational schedule provides an internal understanding of time, people, and materials needed to produce the service or products.

The flow-on effect of materials and labour management can directly affect the work schedule. Just-in-time availability of materials delivery and temporary staffing from agencies can be a blessing as well as a trap when it comes to meeting the scheduled time. For operations that are heavily reliant on temporary resources and a fixed schedule, last-minute changes can add unnecessary workload and stress when the availability isn't fulfilling the needs of the scheduled production.

Sales and demand fluctuations add to the complexity of time management. An expected change might be a new business contract with wholesalers of bulk volume or a promotional effort to boost volume. As expected, they are included in the increased workload. The surge in demand might result from media and celebrity exposure or a change of freight schedule, but those changes cannot guarantee the same schedule delivery expectations.

External changes often happen unexpectedly. Ideally, the operational schedule should be closely monitored and adjusted as needed to reduce the flow-on impact of production and customer expectations. The foreseeable changing factors, such as weather forecasts that may disrupt transport, can be incorporated into the planning and the operational schedule in advance with built-in flexibility.

> Operating a dynamic operational schedule that is flexible, agile and scalable is like opening an umbrella to meet the needs of the end-users. It is the way to improve performance amidst the uncertain forecast.

Imagine an operation schedule as an umbrella. We expect the umbrella to open and protect us from the weather when we pull the trigger. If the umbrella opens on time when it rains, we get the most out of the structural mechanism, and it works precisely to meet our needs.

Let's consider the on-time and on-schedule performance of the operations through the umbrella analogy:

What if we wanted to open the umbrella, but it did not work? In this case, the operation schedule could not respond to the customer demand due to structural issues and therefore could not meet the customer's needs.

What if we did not want the umbrella to open yet it opened unexpectedly? Early or unexpected delivery from the operational schedule may not please the customer. That is particularly so when the goods or services provided are time-bound with food safety or security requirements. Operating a dynamic operational schedule that is flexible, agile and scalable is like opening an umbrella to meet the needs of the end-users. It is the way to improve performance amidst the uncertain forecast.

Case study: ABC Enterprise Forward Planning

ABC Enterprise has a regular schedule of outbound freight every day at 9pm, so the goods can be transported across the network to be delivered nationwide the following day.

In early December, demand for transporting goods increases because of the Christmas holiday season. It is entirely in line with the expectations of the operations team, as they've experienced the surge of workload first-hand in the past. Knowing the daily schedule in advance, the team understands that forward planning is critical to the operation's success during the busy season.

Months before December, the operations team has already received the sales and demand forecast from their sales and finance teams, and they've adjusted the ongoing operational workload analysis. The HR team has data from the previous Christmas holiday staffing records and has already started considering the temporary adjustments on the current roster. The operation team has gathered and consolidated the data from various departments to provide feedback to the operations manager as part of the operation planning process.

The operations management team and the leaders on the floor have assessed staff availability for the updated peak season roster, which the operation planning and HR teams can now use to ensure that the people resource is scalable when the workload surges. This includes rostering a mix of part-time and casual staff for the busy hours. The team has arranged for external agencies as a backup plan and has already discussed staff requirements throughout the busy season to ensure temporary staffing is available if needed. They conducted extra training, so the internal team is cross-trained to move between different pockets of operations.

Not surprisingly, with this level of forward planning in place and the built-in agility of the team, the surge of workload had little impact on the performance of the operations team. The daily freight departed with confidence that the goods would be delivered to the distribution centre for on-time delivery to customers.

The peak season roster met the demand without significant unplanned overtime, and external agencies provided temporary staff after some unexpected staff availability issues. The operations team could focus on getting their jobs done, knowing that they were well resourced to cope with the additional workload. Extra staffing was available to support internally and externally if needed. There was a sense of satisfaction and accomplishment having completed another successful busy holiday season in operations and knowing the business had come together to make it happen.

Compliance

According to the Merriam-Webster online dictionary, *compliance* means the act or process of complying with a desire, demand, proposal, regimen, or coercion, as well as conformity in fulfilling official requirements and a disposition to yield to others.

My own painful experiences with compliance policies and activities suggest that getting people to follow the standard ways of working can feel like a forceful act. I can confidently say that compliance is not a favourite word for most people in the operations sector.

> I can confidently say that compliance is not a favourite word for most people in the operations sector.

Despite that, compliance is essential for manufacturing and logistics operations. It ensures the ongoing safety and security of the products, services, company assets, and the people involved in the process. With early detection, compliance checks and audits uncover business risks and educate the team to apply best practices to any issues. They raise awareness as well as the quality standards of work delivered.

To sum up, here are three layers of manufacturing and logistics compliance with examples. The list provides a taste of what is involved, although it is not an exhaustive list of the standards applicable to your business.

International compliance standards with external auditing. These include:

→ International quality standards applicable by industry, such as ISO standards on manufacturing, machinery, transportation and logistics

→ Food standards, including the U.S. Food and Drug Administration (FDA), European Food Safety Authority (EFSA), and Food and Agriculture Organization of the United Nations

→ The international aviation standards

→ International postal union standards

→ International financial reporting standards.

Compliance and regulations based on local authorities' requirements, including:

→ Infrastructure, building compliance standards

→ Employment and human resources compliance

→ Financial and legal compliance with local regularity

→ Food, health and safety

→ Environmental and sustainability regulatory.

Company-wide compliance standards ensure efficiency and consistency across a geographically-distributed network, including:

→ Environmental

→ Social responsibility and governance

→ Digital systems

- ➜ Technologies governance
- ➜ Other internal standards.

Regulatory legislation documents can be challenging to read and understand – even for professionals in their respective fields. It will be a game-changer if the management team can digest and translate compliance requirements into relevant, everyday language for the wider business to understand and follow.

Efficiency and bottom-line revenue

Operational performance data

We've explored financial profitability and the operational performance indicators separately. Now let's look at how they combine to contribute to the operational performance and impact the bottom-line revenue.

Setting up performance indicators is only the start of improving operational performance. Many outstanding factors can impact and cause data fluctuation. System configuration constraints, the team's understanding of the data entry process, their availability to enter data manually, system automation integration issues during automatic data capturing, the timing of the reporting, and others. All can influence the accuracy of the data.

The financial reporting team regularly analyses the performance data with commentary and investigates the drivers behind the numbers. If consistent symptoms are impacting the data, then additional attention is needed to find the root causes. It is useful to conduct operational diagnostics with a subject matter expert to better understand the operational performance and the impact on bottom-line revenue.

Operational performance and diagnostics

An operation is like a toddler. The data we've gathered so far in the financial and operational performance is like the numbers from the child's health check report. The performance numbers themselves don't mean a lot unless we care about the person's health. We care far more if it is someone we love and who is close to us.

Performance numbers can be perceived in many ways without understanding what they mean. Think of a time when the operational cost dropped unexpectedly and bounced back again the next month without apparent reason. Did different teams come up with varying interpretations? Was there a satisfactory explanation at the end? Everyone involved has their own perception of why things happened and what contributed to the fluctuation in the results.

There are several reasons why we need thorough operational diagnostics with a subject matter expert. They act as an independent pair of eyes to support performance improvement.

Firstly, the operations team is deeply involved and forms opinions based on experience. Love is blind, and so are people who only believe their perception.

Second, exposure to a single part of the operations may not help those people form a constructive view of the whole operation at a high level.

And third, even though the team can have a helicopter view of the end-to-end operation, there are blindspots because they are used to their idea of the setup. We cannot know what we don't know. Having an internal team solely in charge of the operational improvement will not deliver the desired outcome – not because they don't care, but because there are natural limitations on how far they can see.

My story

I often had a runny nose and breathing problems as a young child. My parents didn't see it as a health problem, so the symptoms persisted until I got pneumonia and had to check into the hospital. Back in the 1980s, the hospital tied children (particularly active toddlers like me) to their beds to ensure their safety and recovery. It was probably one of the worst experiences of my life.

Once the pneumonia was clear, I was discharged, and life essentially went back to normal. Others might have noticed that I had other minor symptoms such as chest pain and wheezing during exercise, but I simply lived with it.

I finally got a correct diagnosis from another medical professional more than ten years later when I realised that my breathing was louder than others. It turned out I have a mild case of asthma. The diagnosis helps me dispel some of my perceptions. My constant tiredness wasn't from being lazy, a health condition caused it, and I now have tools to maintain my energy levels.

I often use the child analogy when working with teams because the dynamic of a sick child in the family is similar to when an operation has trouble with its performance. Without knowledge, parents miss obvious symptoms. When word spreads, the wider family gets involved in support without understanding the household routine. Sometimes, the extended family (a grandmother or uncle) knows enough to recognise the child's symptoms and return them to good health, but it isn't always the case, and you can imagine the drama and tension of different family members' opinions.

We cannot expect a small child to perform to expected standards unless we understand the obstacles they are facing. The child does not have the awareness or the voice to speak and explain the problems. At this point, we need tools to understand the underlying cause of the symptoms.

Chinese medical principles have been useful in diagnosing the health of an operational business. There are four core parts of the Chinese medical diagnostic: observing, smelling, inquiring and treating.

I have modified those principles with some additional steps to become operational diagnostics. Here are the steps and insights on the method of diagnostics.

Operational Diagnostics

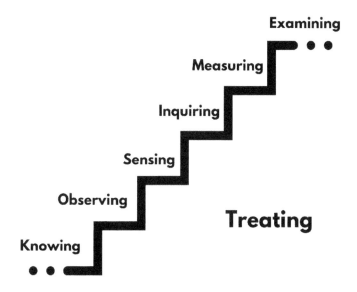

Figure 5: Operational diagnostics

Knowing is awareness of the symptoms or performance data that points to the area of attention. As in my personal health story, there's no action until we recognise that something needs to be done. If you were at the medical centre, you would have explained your symptoms at this point.

Observing and **Sensing** involve looking at the environment with an open mind to gather information and understanding. Observing the cleanliness, the physical setup, and the movement of people and goods can provide cues about the status quo. Sense or scan emotions to understand the dynamics of the teams involved.

The long-term health of the operation depends on the ability of caregivers to share the responsibility as a team and to conduct routine tasks with care and confidence. Don't jump to conclusions at this point, as we are only skimming the surface. For example, a medical professional would look at your overall appearance to understand your health status and consider underlying issues.

Inquiring is further exploring the perception and gathering qualitative facts on the situation. Besides the performance results, what are our experiences to date? What do we perceive is working well? What isn't going well? Is there a particular area that is causing more grief than others? At a medical check-up, having the person explain their health status helps the medical expert understand the person's awareness. A small child would need an immediate family member to answer those questions.

Measuring with focus on the operation and **Examining** the needs. By now, we have narrowed the area to be considered. We can gather specific operations data and determine if they support our early perception. Imagine that at this point, the medical professional might be asking for a particular test and samples to support an early diagnosis.

Some root causes might require an additional examination to gather more information. For a business, that could mean further baseline testing and analysis with manual or automated processes. With a summary of reports and understanding, the symptoms and the possible root causes may become apparent, and treatment can be prescribed to reduce the shared discomfort and improve the setup.

Ways to leak profit

Once the operation's health is determined, it is time to identify the specific treatment to improve the outcomes. With so many moving parts, it is quite possible to have a gap or two in the process. Those are where we see efficiency and profit leakage.

Many of us have heard of the Toyota Production Systems (TPS) philosophy to eliminate waste in the production process. The original seven forms of waste (Muda) that are part of the TPS are Transportation, Inventory, Motion, Waiting, Overproduction, Overprocessing, and Defects (Kubiak & Benbow, 2007).

Imagine the water pipes as the operation, and the goal is to create electricity by moving water through a series of water wheels. We can reinterpret water as resources, materials, and people hours that go through the system to create value for others. The less leakage of resources, the more power will be generated.

Transportation

The job of pipes is to transport water, so we want it to flow through as efficiently as possible in a single direction. That sounds simple and sensible, yet it is not easy in an operational context.

Being closely involved on an operation floor can make it more difficult to see how the materials and people move back and forth. To obtain clarity (particularly if the operation is geographically distributed), draw the direction of the transport, time involved, and transportation activities of goods and services in a graphic visual to demonstrate their impact on the outcome.

One technique used in Lean management is called Value Stream Mapping. Previously, it required manual data gathering to build up the whole story of time, place, and transport movement. With more sophisticated tracking and Internet of Things (IoT) technologies, we can gather real-time data to provide a 24/7 understanding of where, when, and possibly how transportation impacts performance.

Inventory

Too much stock on hand equals holding money that cannot be liquidated. Water that is blocked and not flowing to where it is needed can become dead water. The inventory inside the system creates a blockage and can potentially damage other parts of the process. Insufficient inventory means not enough revenue will be generated, making it difficult to maintain momentum.

During the pandemic, disruption of the global supply chain has slowed the supply of non-essential products through manufacturing and distribution networks. The flow-on effect of such wide-scale disruption is difficult to comprehend; hence, it is more important than ever to monitor, forecast, and control the inventory and ideally build more agility in production planning. Digital and real-time technology can be leveraged to support the forecasting and monitoring process.

Motion

Often, operational components move simultaneously with little awareness of the purpose. Imagine constantly moving the pipes and the joints of your water supply at home. The more change, the less likely you will have water – until you stop muddling the setup.

It is similar in the physical setup of the operation and process. In large scale production, it can be the arrangement of the functions or, on a smaller scale, the design of a one-person workstation. Either way, any other motion that does not add value is a cost that will reduce profitability. Automating physical configuration and digital monitoring helps minimise unnecessary movement.

Waiting

Imagine that the water pipes are clear, but someone still needs to turn on the tap. For whatever reasons (water restrictions enforcement, an upstream issue of a watergate, or the tap setup), the remaining water pipes won't function or generate the required power.

In a complex operation, the waiting game can be obscure. It might be a supply department issue with vendor delay, approval for work needed or, as in the water example, the physical setup of having people and transport ready to ship things out. Waiting can be incredibly frustrating for the team, especially when it results from a lack of planning and miscommunication. Upfront planning, scheduling, and real-time monitoring progress are important to reduce the waiting time.

Overproduction

Having too much isn't always a good thing and can cost the operation dearly. Overproduction of electricity can lead to storage issues and wastage when there is no demand. The customer has committed to goods and services in a fixed price service contract or forecasting estimation. While it is wise to have a slight buffer to ensure production meets changing demand, over-production means an increase in labour, materials, and overheads with no increase in sales. Avoid overproduction by closely monitoring daily production and operation plans, performance indicators, and daily financial results.

Overprocessing

The scale of water pipes can be overly complicated to service water flow towards the hydropower generator and thus reduce the output flow. Operational examples include some logistical operations with many checkpoints and depot processing. In manufacturing, the problem is over-servicing and exceeding the customers' needs at the expense of the business's time and effort.

To avoid over-processing, we need to look at the agreed service level for external customers and regularly review internal process touchpoints to ensure the work does not exceed the requirements. Regular performance discussions, better communication of those requirements and expectations, and performance goal-setting embed a good level of quality while not over-processing or over-delivering.

Defects

Debris in water blocks the pipes, reducing the flow and, worst of all, creating problems in the infrastructure and further reducing electricity generation performance. It's the same with defects in materials and supply. The upfront quality control of the supply is significant as a gatekeeping mechanism for the rest of the operation.

While it is essential to ensure quality inputs, the importance of having a well-designed manufacturing system and processes cannot be understated. An example is the quality of materials that meet customer requirements, such as the heat tolerance of a plastic mould and precise measurement for purposeful fitting. Logistical services require quality information input and the item received on time to process the expected outcome and delivery time accurately. Resolving the problem of defects requires a systematic approach that starts where the defects are found and analyses the impact from up and downstream.

Which of the seven points above are the most relevant for your environment? Is there an obvious one that has the most impact on the business's health and profit?

The value of communication

It would be great to simply put individuals together and have them converge into a happy and productive team. But we live in reality, and there are no magic bullets for teams. The way to ensure that individuals work toward a common goal is through communication. It is an essential quality of operational health that is often overlooked.

Imagine a group of people asked to draw part of a table without instruction. The resulting pictures will likely show tables of entirely different shapes, sizes, or parts. Some might be comfortable drawing the whole table, while others might decide to be creative and design a floating tabletop.

> There are no magic bullets for teams.

Suppose we translate that example to the scale of a nationwide and global operation network. In that case, it is not difficult to understand the hardship and frustration people face in meeting performance requirements. How much time and effort is wasted through a lack of clear communication in the workplace?

Communication is an essential tool in improving bottom-line revenue. Sandra Cleary's book *Communication: A Hands-on Approach* offers a circular model to describe the communication between the sender and the audience. When the sender shares a message, the message is encoded to make the idea accessible via verbal, visual, and physical body language. The audience receives and decodes the idea of the message.

When both groups share a similar understanding and worldview, there is a good chance that the message will be decoded and understood with the original intent (Cleary, 2004). A simple case of signalling danger can be shared differently, depending on the sender's background and how the audience interprets the message. The purpose and the context of communication are important in interpersonal communication within the team.

We need to look at organisational communication to ensure individuals work together across the business. Cleary suggests that the management of an organisation impacts the directions and channels of communication, as does the way we structure teams. Consider their functions, roles, and responsibility when it comes to communications. Cleary's four directions and channels within the organisation are upwards, downwards, lateral (sideways), and informal (grapevine).

Managing communications in operations requires purposeful downwards communication and messages fed upward from the frontline team. This two-way communication forms a feedback loop to bind the teams with increased understanding. Continuous two-way communication provides good awareness of the operation's health from the top to the frontline.

Mind your head with the overheads

Understanding overheads

Managing overhead costs has always been a high priority for executives in the manufacturing industry and will be an even hotter topic as we emerge into a new normal.

In a cross-industries survey in 2009, McKinsey found that companies have generated savings of up to 50 per cent in their manufacturing processes through lean manufacturing techniques. Many, however, were yet to tap into overhead cost opportunities in warehousing and transportation that can generate 20 to 50 per cent savings (Alicke & Lösch, 2010).

Despite past efforts to streamline the warehousing and transportation process, ongoing irregularity in the global supply chain and logistics network means warehousing and transportation across the global supply chain will continue to be costly and challenging.

The manufacturing overhead cost contains expenses other than direct materials and direct labour. With this in mind, overhead costs contribute to a large portion of the company's expenditure. This makes it essential to analyse overheads when it comes to the Voice of Business (VoB) and improving profitability.

Shared administration and indirect labour costs sit across various departments and functions. Accountability for overheads resides with the financial controller and the business unit's executive to oversee the activities and expenses.

The reality is that no single person can have complete oversight and control over the granular overhead expenditures of the operation and business at the enterprise level. Therefore, transparency of the spending, ownership of the delegation, and a clear process will ensure the team collaborates with shared responsibility.

Examples of the overhead cost items:

- ➜ General administration of office and sites management, cost accounting, supervisors, and shared services staff.

- ➜ Infrastructure, facilities, equipment, and utility costs, such as lease, rent, depreciation of tools, plant equipment, and insurance. Electricity and water can be huge cost contributors for process-based industries. Historical survey data showed electricity accounts for about 4 per cent of the total manufacturing cost of an average plant in machinery industries (Miller & Vollmann, 1985).

- ➜ Material overhead costs related to procurement, transportation, coordination of warehouses, and logistics.

- ➜ Indirect labour includes the wages of hourly workers who are not directly involved in the manufacturing and production of goods and services. Staff dedicated to materials handling, maintenance, and quality control are in this category.

A process flow chart is an engaging way to discuss overhead costs with the team across departments. Seeing the cost and the activities visually provides an understanding of how the dollar values relate to day-to-day tasks. For example, an administration cost can be an overhead that needs reviewing. Once an activity has been identified, a more focused approach to understanding the finer details will provide further insights into the overheads involved. Office supplies can make up an unusually large proportion of administrative costs. This information provides the team with a direction to further understand the cause of overhead cost increase and find a potential remedy.

Case study: Woody

Woody, a home decor manufacturer, is part of an international lifestyle business that budgets raw materials as direct material costs and the woodworkers as direct labour.

The overhead costs are administrative salaries, administrative payroll taxes, machinery depreciation, the cost to lease the workshop, travel, and utilities such as electricity. As a branch of an international business, there is an additional cost to the local and global management structure.

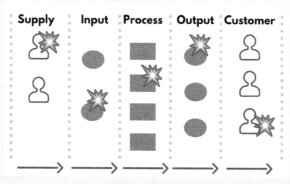

Figure 6: Illustration of overhead cost items in SIPOC analysis

From a helicopter view, each of the icons in figure 6 represents an overhead cost item, with the sparks representing the spending at Woody. Several overhead cost items can be better managed. With the process visualisation, it is possible to review the cost associated with the activities and uncover ways to streamline and increase efficiencies. The executive team can track and prioritise which overhead items and activities need reviewing by providing a regular snapshot of the overhead costs in the business process. It has resulted in a continuous pipeline of savings.

Maintenance matters

For manufacturing, logistics, and process-based industries, the ability to acquire buildings, equipment infrastructure, and the network brings significant competitive advantages in the global market.

While it is nice to have the network and infrastructure, the reality is that they are only useful when well-utilised for commercial purposes. The machinery, equipment, and plant availability depend on how well they are maintained over time. According to the *Physical Asset Management Handbook*, the historical benchmark availability of the manufacturing plant should be greater than 97 per cent (Mitchell, 2002). It is clear that management, to date, still holds this benchmark in practice where possible.

Achieving a high level of availability requires a relatively heavy workload and upfront cost in maintaining and sustaining the infrastructure. Even though many operations face challenges, it is crucial to meet infrastructure maintenance requirements to remain a commercial advantage rather than a financial liability.

Infrastructure maintenance is much more than keeping the lights on. This area is heavily involved in the risk and cost management of the operations. An overview of the infrastructure maintenance responsibilities are:

- building maintenance and compliance procedures
- equipment, electrical compliance procedures, and setup safety mechanism in machinery
- understanding health and safety regulations through local and international authority rules where applicable
- understanding international regulations and requirements is part of the facility management responsibility. Logistics include Universal Postal Union's Universal Postal Conventions and Regulations, International Postal Corporation Standards and International Civil Aviation Organization on international and security regulations
- proactive planning in depreciation and replacement of equipment and parts
- managing the infrastructure, connectivity, and monitoring of utility (energy consumption, water usage, gas and other chemicals)
- collaboration with management in the design and installation of health and safety, security systems
- regular proactive inspection and maintenance

- ➔ risk and issue registration logging and resolving in the work management system

- ➔ maintenance team management

- ➔ collaboration on utility cost savings and sustainability initiatives

- ➔ management of the sub-contractors and their delivered outcomes

- ➔ additionally, some maintenance departments look after the transportation fleet and maintenance depending on the structure.

The ongoing challenges of the maintenance team are limited resources of staff trained with specific technicality, controlling the cost while delivering outcomes, and access to data from various systems and sources. The challenges escalate further when subcontracting companies collapse, leaving a shortage of parts from overseas, as well as a potentially deeper talent shortage in the local market.

There are many ways to improve the cost-effectiveness of infrastructure maintenance.

Review the maintenance management model

Understand whether an in-house team, an outsourced model, or a hybrid maintenance task force may be more effective with the specific infrastructure needs. While an in-house team appears to be cost-efficient, there is a level of training and development involved. Speciality skills in a particular subject matter area can be acquired but are challenging to retain in a highly competitive job market for trading staff.

Proactive maintenance to reduce cost

A well-oiled machine will likely run a lot smoother for longer with less friction and wear. Ensure upfront planning across the machinery and sites so the team is always on top of their game. Scheduling preventative maintenance lightens the team's load to gather information and determine which and what to maintain. With the current shortage of materials and uncertainty of contractor availability, planning reduces the chances of emergency callout fees and not having the right parts to get a maintenance job done.

Learn from SMED to reduce production downtime

SMED is a concept that originates from reducing the downtime in replacing consumables in printing machines. It was developed to optimise machine usage in the 1950s in Japan. Noting which step causes the most lost time during a changeover of machine consumables and setup means we can streamline the tasks by reviewing the activity required, eliminating or reducing unnecessary movement, and potentially setting up parallel operations to enable continuity of production.

Mistake prevention to reduce unnecessary workload

There are already enough day-to-day tasks on the plate of the operations and the maintenance team. Unexpected and unnecessary breakdowns due to human error are hugely frustrating for the team and the production schedule. We can apply mistake prevention techniques to avoid undesirable actions.

Start the process by taking stock of high impact recurrence mistakes

How were they discovered? Where was the mistake made? From here, we can apply Cause-Effect analysis tools, such as the Ishikawa (also called the Fishbone Diagram) and the Five Whys Cause and Effect Chain.

Deciding which tools are most suitable depends on the team's exposure and understanding in real-life situations. Some tools have helpful categories, such as machines, people and systems, and identify how they impact the outcomes. It helps the team consider and brainstorm the potential causes. Through team validation and iteration, chances are a solution will be found to prevent mistakes.

Effective organisational structure to enable collaboration across the function

The maintenance function often sits with the finance department or the operations team. Given the level of financial authority delegation, there is a good chance that a business case is required to justify a significant project installation or a fix of the operation's assets. Having structure and clarity of process enables cooperation across departments and reduces the approval waiting time across the whole maintenance function.

Break silos for greater resources

*'Silos – and the turf wars
they enable – devastate
organizations. They waste
resources, kill productivity,
and jeopardize the
achievement of goals.'*

– Patrick Lencioni (Lencioni, 2006).

A physical silo is a storage infrastructure, while a functioning silo infrastructure has a designated input and a specific volume for the storage and output channels. The purpose of a silo is to keep goods and materials in storage and distribute bulk material with less manual effort. A well-planned silo keeps valuable resources safe and brings logistical efficiency.

Unlike physical storage, siloed teams that do not cooperate or share knowledge cause rework, create frustration and bring down employee morale. Think of a time when a department has made changes that impact everyone else without considering the impact on the customers and consequences to the business. Multiply this action with the number of departments and locations across the organisation. Siloed teams create endless fires to put out. All that unnecessary wasted effort could have significantly improved profitability.

Research estimates that the Fortune 500 companies lose at least US$31.5 billion annually by failing to share knowledge (Quast, 2012). It also indicates that organisations worldwide have sunk billions of dollars in implementing knowledge management systems since the 1990s, trying to resolve the barrier of knowledge sharing – all with minimal results.

A colleague told me of a cement silo that broke in Auckland, New Zealand, some years ago, and the team that spent many weeks cleaning up the mess it created across the city. We certainly don't want that kind of broken silo.

What does it mean to break team silos? It ensures the team recognises their unique contribution and knows they need to be transparent in their work and connected to the rest of the organisation. Cooperating and sharing knowledge as part of a team is a shared responsibility. Resolving problems will be easier and more efficient if the parties work together (despite being different).

If working together is so good, why do teams operate in silos? Understandably, the human mind does what makes it feel secure. Chances are, keeping the resources and information within an enclosed, rigid area of control can appear to bring comfort and political power. That false sense of security comes at the expense of the rest of the team and customers.

We can resolve team silos by fostering an understanding of the impact of their actions on the business and the customers. Refresh the ground rules and shared values to help the team reflect and align with the company. To build on that, recognise that individual and group contributions are essential, with expertise and differences as key ingredients bringing strength to the business.

The organisational structure is another reason why teams operate in silos. Rigid hierarchies, team structures, and processes lead to bottlenecks. It may also be that the structure failed to recognise a team's limited capacity, so the team had to create a way to manage its workload.

Observations and data gathering can help identify the bottleneck and understand how a silo is formed. You can resolve structural silos by having executive sponsorship commit to resolving the potential issue, facilitating an open dialogue, growing the team's problem-solving capability, and improving the transparency of cross-functional processes.

The lack of systems and process synchronisation is another reason multiple silos are seen across the organisation. This is probably one of the bigger issues for the operational team due to the lack of investment in continual process improvement and fragmented technologies implementation.

A thorough analysis and system investigation can locate gaps in the intersection of systems and processes. Check with the team on their pain points to validate their needs. With system information and team feedback, quick wins and Kaizen improvement initiatives can be identified to eliminate the issues for long-term business benefits.

Innovation and profitability

Why do we bother with innovation? Is it improving efficiency, creating new commercial opportunities, or keeping up with trendy technologies that meet customer needs?

During the pandemic, companies have had to quickly implement remote working technologies and find new ways to digitalise the manual process, given ongoing social restrictions and lockdown. Global software company Twilio has found that 97 per cent of the 2,569 enterprise decision-makers surveyed said the pandemic sped up their digital transformation, and 79 per cent said their digital change budget had increased (Koetsier, 2020).

McKinsey's 2020 global survey found that technology adoption has accelerated seven years since the pandemic started (McKinsey, 2020). Statistics tell us there's only a 30 per cent success rate in complex, large-scale digital technology transformation, and most do not meet their stated goals (McKinsey, 2019). The trend is likely to continue due to common pitfalls such as lack of team engagement, poor collaboration and lack of accountability with little support by the management (Bucy et al., 2020).

A significant increase in demand and a limited pool of IT talent globally add salt to the wound. The new trend has triggered a rise in IT salary resources on top of the skill shortage. It is even more challenging to get things done.

The trouble is that large and complex digital and business transformations often try to change the core of the business by force, not by nature. That includes changing the business model, supplementing by designing and implementing the technology to drive changes in people's behaviour. While it can be due to a vision to future proof the business, it often comes from an egotistic drive to create achievement in the short term, within the limited terms of the decision-makers.

Ambitious and untested goals force changes to happen quickly, regardless of which stage of the business growth cycle the business is in. It is like putting all the ingredients of a stew into a pressure cooker to force it to cook quickly. While it is possible to tenderise and cook meat quickly using the pressure method, it is not applicable to speed up technology implementation and the people involved by pressurising it. There is no shortcut to real transformation.

> There is no shortcut to real transformation.

Innovate to evolve

We need a new perspective to avoid being one of many failed digital transformations. Forget change and transformation altogether. Changes made to us are orders and instructions to do things differently. Transformation does not happen unless you are born with the DNA to transform from a caterpillar to a butterfly. You can't be something you are not.

We can, however, harness our power to create, innovate and evolve the business and technology. Scientists and artists have moments of insight and transform their work naturally. The cumulative effort can lead to a significant breakthrough. Whether software in code or hardware in physical form, the technologies are no different from an artist's tools. Innovating and evolving an existing business smartly with technology is the challenge for tomorrow's executives. Honest iterations with integrity in the decision and planning process will safeguard the evolutionary journey.

The journey almost always starts with the ideation of the vision. The ideation process must align with the strategic and operational needs and financial justification to proceed with innovation. Instead of coming up with a big, fat business case, a one-page business model will indicate the necessary understanding of the purpose and alignment of the innovation to the overall business strategy. It needs regular review and refinement.

Some innovative ideas and technologies are more expensive up front, but the commercial benefit outweighs the cost in the long term. A cross-functional decision-making panel can represent the voice across the business to review ideas against a set of agreed criteria to ensure the accepted innovations are fit for purpose.

Implementing fragmented technologies across the operation creates an ongoing financial and technical burden for the business. Some technology innovation decisions are made by decision-makers with histories. The technologies are implemented without assessing why they are needed and how they will work in the unique environment of the new normal. Proactive development and management of the technology strategy aligned with business needs will prevent the existing issues from snowballing into a large financial liability.

Case study: Part I – ABC Enterprise's innovation programme

As a service business that provides printed learning resources, ABC Enterprise is considering using innovation and technology to transform the customer experience and implement new operating models within two years. The goal is to align with growing customer needs on mobile devices and engage more commercially with new and existing customers to increase sales revenue.

Leaders in ABC Enterprise have come up with several projects to digitalise their manual services to meet the brief. Individually, projects are drafted, scoped, and implemented with reporting to the board of directors. A new customer experience journey has been created alongside some existing customers' wish lists. In the future, new and current customers will be able to access services and products via online channels, with less reliance on contact centre staff or account managers.

Because the operation has always been manual with little technology, the company has little spare IT resources or knowledge to proceed with the technology programme. It has had to recruit contractors such as IT project managers, analysts, and technical vendors to support its move to digital. They report to their departmental leaders with progress and suggestions of technologies to replace the paper-based processes.

Several new software and technology platforms have been investigated and recommendations made to the leaders. Some of the proposed technologies can deliver amazing capabilities, which has excited the board of directors. Funding was released with strict requirements on the delivery timeline.

Upon proceeding, it appears that several cross-functional procedures need reviewing before some digital technologies can be put in place. As the project progresses, more critical infrastructure issues are identified. Before implementing new applications, some basic infrastructure functions and standards must be established to ensure a stable foundation.

It was also discovered that individual projects have many cross-functional touchpoints that were ignored when scoping the minimum viable implementation. The legacy system that was to be scrapped had functionalities that would have cost a fortune for another provider to develop. It would also have required a significant change in how things are done. Delay on the timeline was inevitable, and the programme cost increased. The innovation programme intended to deliver new commercial revenue and improved customer experience suddenly became a significant burden for the business.

Is the technology a good fit?

Investment in changing technology can bring benefits or disasters. It largely depends on whether the chosen solution is fit for purpose.

In larger enterprises, a technology director may understand business requirements and support others to implement the differences in technology solutions. The benefit is the oversight and potential better alignment of the technologies with the strategic alignment. The problem is that there could be a barrier to innovation and technology investment if the single party in charge of all technologies is not on board.

With some companies moving away from a single leadership position having oversight of the strategy and operations of technologies, the financial and operations teams are increasingly important in choosing the right technology for the business.

Having worked mostly in non-IT roles, these teams face challenges well outside their knowledge domain. They have to juggle their day-to-day responsibilities and expectations to make the right decisions and implement the new system. With little time and limited knowledge, it is no surprise that the financial and operational teams can find it difficult to fully comprehend the pros and cons of new technology during the consultation process with the providers.

There are twelve steps to select technology that better fits the needs of the business operation.

1. Allow time to embrace the new idea
2. Do not rush and decide on change and innovation that has little buy-in
3. Create a safe space for open discussion of needs
4. Ensure the changes address both internal and external needs of the business
5. Understand the strategy and process now and for the future

6. Consider present and future needs jointly for coherent consistency

7. Use animation and story to explain the various technologies options in plain language

8. Engage the wider team with creative storytelling and technologies to help them absorb and understand the possibilities in the workplace and the business

9. Engage a trusted technical and operational advisor to provide independent advice on design and implementation

10. Align the technology selection with operations now and in the future

11. Apply joint decision-making processes across the functions

12. Make information transparent to support a thorough understanding of the joint decision-making process.

Invest technology wisely

As common sense would have it, if there is already a billing system in place, you probably are not going to need to double the work and pay for another one. Implementing a critical system infrastructure is not the same as buying another pair of shoes for a different outing. The price of investing in such core technology will be a single solution for all occasions.

Yet, many businesses are still paying the price of choosing multiple technologies that provide similar functionality.

Here is a process to ensure the technology investment is spent wisely.

1. Understand the aspirations of innovation and the critical success factors

2. Make sure the implementation team fully understands the importance of current functionalities

3. Formulate the non-negotiable needs in the new system

4. Validate business-critical functionalities with a live demonstration and a copy of data similar to the real process

5. Develop robust decision-making processes to establish critical success factors are met.

Enterprise process architecture

The business strategy informs an enterprise process architecture in an ideal scenario, where strategic directions are streamlined into several functions and operations. The enterprise architecture explains how strategic goals will be achieved and which team is responsible for specific outcomes. In plain English, the enterprise process architecture is a way to design activities that will form a consistent approach to achieving business results. It usually shares an alignment with the financial reporting structure.

In our increasingly complex business environment, changes to operations happen at lightning speed. Manually tracking processes have been deemed impossible and therefore neglected to prioritise day-to-day activities and meet performance objectives.

The downside of not understanding the enterprise process architecture is the amount of time and cost to work out logically how the innovation and technologies can be put in place and performed in the operation where the certainty of compliance and on-time delivery is needed.

Adapting the Agile business model offers increased flexibility in the continuous iteration of process and delivery. The enterprise process architecture looks much more like a living distributed network of teams with shared responsibility and system ownership. Gone are the days of having stacks of static process manuals; instead, we have a repository of living and breathing documentation that continues to evolve. Investing resources and the technology to understand the status quo will be beneficial in aligning the new strategy with how the functional teams operate differently in the new era. This enables better operation performance understanding and delivers innovation in the long run.

Alignment of digital architecture and business processes

In theory, the technical team that manages the digital systems infrastructure has multiple pictures describing how the current systems and data work together. These are often referred to as technical systems architecture diagrams.

The rest of the business may be unaware of these diagrams because they are highly technology-focused. However, the information should be shared and discussed during the discovery phase of a company-wide technology change. It will ensure that cross-functional team members share an understanding of the flow of information and data from the operational actions.

It is an opportunity for the operation team to give feedback to the technical team on their day-to-day operational actions and for the technical team to provide clarity around the system functionality. This small piece of work can potentially resolve some common issues, strengthen the collaboration and possibly even speed up the implementation of the new systems. Working with transparency and constant feedback loops reduces resistance to innovation borne of fear and uncertainty, so the team can focus on ironing out any implementation issues.

Case study: Part II – ABC Enterprise Innovation Programme

Continuing the earlier story, the innovation programme of ABC Enterprise had come to a tipping point, needing a full review because of outdated technology infrastructure. The enterprise processes were not aligned with the original understanding, thus causing a significant delay in delivery. Continuing the innovation programme would hurt current clients and add pressure to the operation.

The board of directors and the leadership team had independently reviewed the innovation programme, and clear actions were taken:

- Review the enterprise strategy and prioritise the desired outcomes.
- Reset the scope and timeline of the innovation programme to be more aligned with the resource level and set a realistic pace of change for the business operation.
- Strengthen the governance steering across both the core business and the innovation programme.
- Review the technical team and resource level to support basic functions and future needs.
- Review fragmented technologies recommended by project teams and across several vendors.

Despite the additional effort of resetting the innovation programme, ABC Enterprise benefited from greater stability and reduced the pressure on the operation team to deliver both day-to-day and innovation initiatives.

The initiatives were completed in a structured way to deliver the expected outcome over a longer period through streamlined enterprise processes and technologies. With strengthened integration of technology and operation, clients could start utilising the new engagement channels in stages. The programme achieved its scope of improving customer engagement and is likely to generate better revenue with the improved customer experience.

PART TWO

THE VOICE OF THE CUSTOMER

Understanding your customer

When understanding the Voice of the Customer, it makes sense to examine some fundamentals. Who are your customers? Who pays for your products and services? How are they paying for it? When do they buy?

It is possible to better understand customers through the sales channels and the data provided. Customers generally come from the three sales channels in the logistics and manufacturing industry.

Direct sales: A retail or an online channel wholly owned by the service manufacturer. The company owns the customer interaction data. An example is a freight company that has its own retail and online channel selling freight services.

Indirect sales: Sales are generated from a third-party platform, either online or retail, selling products and services from various providers and manufacturers. Less customer data is available from the third-party platform. An example is a branded platform that lists packaged food products from various providers to consumers.

Wholesale: Businesses that purchase large quantities of products at low cost. Sales and customer service data is available, but there is limited insight into consumer behaviour. An example is buying health supplements in bulk from the manufacturer to be resold through a retail channel.

The type of sales dictates how much data is available to understand shopping behaviours in-store, the products compared with online stores, and direct feedback channels such as social media accounts.

CHRISTINE W.K. YIP

Understanding the direct sales customers can be a relatively easy task because frequent interactions and data from observations make it possible to build customer personas from the characteristics of real customers.

The idea of building a virtual persona or avatar profile using the characteristics of existing customers enables the team to relate to the characters and, therefore, better identify the customers' habits through research. Those characteristics can include demographic information such as age, gender, language, and ethnicity.

The persona comes in handy in new consumer product design and brand value alignment. It is easier to understand and predict the preferences of real people than it is to interpret statistics. The practice helps the team connect and associate with the likes and dislikes of the particular group. In other words, creating virtual personas from the larger pool of customers provides a clearer understanding of the segments of the overall customer base. Surveys and focus groups can further validate the understanding for more personal insights.

The process for understanding wholesale business customers is different. The wholesaler or manufacturer purchases the product and sells the product or services to the end customers. The wholesaler has the channel and gathers the customer's understanding to proceed with the wholesale purchase. It helps to understand the core values and specific drivers of the wholesale customer. Businesses tend to work together because of value alignment and can complement each other. Regular reports of sales and service data analysis and insights and sharing industry market trends are useful tactics to understand business relationships further.

Moving away from the transactional, joint business partners can provide mutual strategic benefits through sharing the network and resources. Despite being in a supplier relationship, there is potential to work together with a joint venture and share resources in a strategic direction.

One such example was the joint venture of DHL international express courier with local New Zealand CourierPost. The international courier giant wished to expand its network reach in New Zealand, and the local postal group needed a premium service to the rest of the world and monetary investment. By entering into a joint venture, the presence of the DHL network in New Zealand has significantly increased with rebranding the DHL red and yellow colours across a local logistics network. CourierPost's offering of international courier services was enriched with the joint partnership.

A joint business partnership needs to start with honest, upfront expectations of both entities. The agreement sets the boundaries of where the partnership begins and where each remains a stand-alone entity. The Voice of Business generally drives a joint business partnership through mutual strategic benefits and the Voice of the Customer, such as creating additional value by improving service availability.

Hearing and validating the Voice of the Customer

Our world is full of noise. I never realised just how much until I put on a pair of hearing aids. In the beginning, it felt overwhelming to hear all the background noise. Everyday sounds from traffic, chatter, construction, the fridge, the computer fan were incessant.

It takes a while for the brain to learn which noises to filter out and then get used to having them in the background. We keep the channels open to pay attention to useful conversations and process the information.

There are many similarities between my hearing experience and distilling the Voice of the Customer. There is a constant, overwhelming level of data and feedback coming from the customers. The most important conversations can be lost amidst other noises when processing information without deliberate intention and purpose.

Case study: A swimmer's experience

A friend and his family visited a swimming facility and had a poor customer experience. The adult pool was open to the public, but the rest of the facility, including the children's pool, was closed. The swimming pool management policy says that children cannot use swimming aids or floating devices in the adult pool. Being out of their depth meant it was too dangerous for them and other beginner swimmers.

It happened to be a busy Sunday, and there were many families with disappointed children. They had paid the entry fee but did not know that only limited facilities were available. My friend was told the pool closure was publicised online, and swimmers should have checked the website for the latest update. The facility management team felt they followed policies and procedures, but the customers were not pleased.

My friend spoke with the pool management to provide feedback on the spot. He suggested that most swimmers do not check the facility's website before making the trip and that elderly customers were even less likely to do so. He suggested that the staff notify other incoming swimmers so they could decide whether or not to swim in the adult pool. The team took the suggestion on board and started to inform other customers before they paid to enter the pool.

In this case, the team that managed and operated the swimming facility felt they were doing things by the book. They followed a maintenance schedule of the facilities, the management of the information to be published online, and the team kept the adult pool policy strictly in place.

The reality is that following procedures without understanding the customers' needs lead to a poor customer experience. Those experiences aren't usually captured in reporting – even if some customers speak out. The way to ensure a great customer experience is to ensure the team operates the business with the customer in mind. At the pools, that was simply being proactive in explaining customers' options before they paid.

Listen for the collective voice

In an enterprise, customer interactions always cross paths with various services; therefore, a higher-level view of the outcome for the customer is crucial.

Think of a bulk food ingredients delivery service – when it comes to customer feedback, a handful or more points of interest need to be investigated. They may be at the warehouse or the service delivery point. Individually the people at each stage have a customer's perspective and interpretation. The driver's sole focus is on the last mile to the delivery point. The warehouse worker focuses on incoming goods and stock rotation, while the business sales team looks at revenue and customer satisfaction. Each group obtains partial information that is meaningful for their area. That means the collective Voice of the Customer is in pieces rather than understood as one.

That is when the customer's voice gets lost in translation. When the silos take over the voice, a delusion appears as the group tries to close their gap of understanding with limited data. When the customer's feedback is about a delivery delay, transport drivers are pushed to be on time. When the ingredient sent is incorrect, the warehouse team gets the blame. The outcome? Individually, the teams at each interest point work towards improvement, but they will never achieve a better combined outcome.

While it is important to look at feedback, we need to understand what the customers are expressing. What emotions are present? Is it excitement, disappointment, or something stronger? The point is that general contentment does not usually trigger customer feedback. Too often, feedback with strong emotions such as anger or frustration is labelled as negative, and the only goal is praise and positive emotions.

While it is important to win over the customers, negative emotions can indicate customer loyalty and a desire for improvement. Once the tone of the customer's voice is established as a baseline, it becomes easier to identify the uncommon tone that has arisen from a particular situation, such as unexpected service failures or a one-off product defect.

Customers can have difficulty describing an event clearly because of their emotions. That is especially true if the incident severely impacted their life. Imagine the stress on a family desperately waiting for the courier to deliver Power of Attorney documents. It would help to have a personal conversation with the customer rather than relying on technologies to analyse the situation. The personal touch differentiates one provider from another.

Validating the Voice of the Customer is essential – just as we listen to the news and pick up information that is relevant to us. If we have no interest in sport, there is no reason to pay attention to which teams are involved in the Olympics. Understanding the customer's language and validating what is relevant within the business operation helps fine-tune our ability to hear their needs. Are the customers' pain points consistent over time? Is customer feedback data generally pointing towards one or multiple areas of the business operation? It is worthwhile to look at the macro point of view of customer feedback and establish their real interest points.

Case study: Fragrant Food Catering

Fragrant Food Catering provides ready-to-eat packaged food for more than a hundred retailers at schools and universities in a metropolitan area. The customer service team collected feedback and found that 30 per cent of their retailers indicated the food price was too high. The service price point was clearly of interest to the retailers.

Should that lead to a simple price change? Probably not. Food items are generally designed and negotiated in the selection process and bound in a sales contract.

The account manager took steps to validate and qualify what the retailers were trying to express. Were the agreements of services in the contract delivered? What were the understandings of service from the institutes, students, and other patrons? Were there any changes in the expectation due to competition in the area?

Further dialogue with the unhappy retailers found that most had started stocking largely organic fresh food items, expecting that a percentage of image-conscious young people would prefer premium healthier snacks. Yet the selected items were of more adventurous flavours and not popular with the students. The feedback from students was not great, and sales were sluggish, which impacted the overall financial performance of the retailers.

The account manager at Fragrant Food Catering suggested gradually phasing out less popular items. She proactively offered a new range of healthier fast-food options for the retailer to choose from as equivalent menu replacements. With the support of the account manager, the retailers were satisfied with the new selection and saw sales increase.

With customers providing insights, it was easy for the account manager of Fragrant Food Catering to consider qualified, practicable next steps toward resolving the dissatisfaction.

Listen without preconception and agenda

When building new relationships, we need to see past the surface to know the person's true colours. It is the same with customers.

Different perceptions of customers exist regardless of the industry. Those assumptions are based on past experiences and would be fine if there was no change in the demographic and their customers didn't age.

The risk with operating from past assumptions is the possibility of miscommunication and misunderstanding your customers' needs. It is simply arrogant if the customer asked for keto but was offered carbohydrate because you thought you knew what they needed better than they did.

Another pitfall is that the internal agenda trumps the customers' voice. One example is not providing an alternative option in order to maintain a sense of security and safety in the internal team. How often do we see service delivery hours remaining static because that's how internal staffing and operating structures have always worked? Enterprises avoid making radical changes because they fall into the too-hard basket. If the operation cannot cope readily with current demand, the constant firefighting becomes a roadblock to the team aligning with the customers' needs. They simply do not have the leisure to plan and proceed with the steps necessary to be customer-centric.

Technologies can play a crucial role in hearing the Voice of the Customer without biases. Recently I upgraded my old hearing aids to newer technologies. The old technology focused on amplifying the noises in the front – expecting to capture speech face-to-face. But we know that conversations and noises requiring our attention come from different directions.

Upgrading to new technologies means the sound in the environment is captured while Artificial Intelligence (AI) differentiates between my voice, other speech, and white noise. I am not interested in amplifying my voice; I want greater awareness of my surroundings and to hear conversations. As my audiologist says, smarter technologies reduce the brain's internal effort to differentiate and make sense of various sounds. This frees up energy and brainpower to do other, more meaningful work.

Similarly, when analysing customer data and feedback, noise comes from different channels – including sales data, call centre statistics, NPS or other customer satisfaction surveys, and social media channels. Market trends and intelligence can be supplementary and confusing if over-analysed. The larger the enterprise, the more human power spent to make sense of the data from various sources, except that because they are analysed in silos, there is plenty of noise but not a coherent customer voice. The numbers in each channel can vary, but the customer-facing team may not be able to explain why such phenomena occur. Customer insights often come from best guesses and are used to make decisions in revenue generation.

We use bottom-up or top-down approaches to remove the guesswork and identify real insights from customer data.

It is important to integrate and consolidate multi-channel data into a single platform with a bottom-up approach. That does not mean drastically changing the systems; it simply means directing the data feed to be read and analysed in one place. It's like having hearing aids to capture surrounding noises, then identifying and processing the most meaningful feedback via AI technologies. With this in place, it removes internal biases during manual data analysis as well as manual effort in manipulating data for insights.

In a top-down approach, customers work with the team to specify which channels and priorities are most important. This approach is more suited to a business-to-business partnership where customer needs are obvious and need to be prioritised throughout the operations processes.

The Voice of the Customer is captured through collaboration in the design process and service delivery. The data is monitored as part of the service level agreement. Technologies can be applied to reduce time and effort in manually analysing the performance and provide further insights that the team may have missed. Two examples are fridge temperature monitoring technologies that ensure frozen food is stored to assure food safety and the geospatial data of signature-required delivery for delivery routes.

Combining process data with customer feedback data provides solid insights from a single view rather than having the teams personally make sense of them and loosely discuss the numbers with their best guesses.

Customers don't know your operation

First impressions of the MTR subway in Hong Kong are of the cleanliness of the station and a payment mechanism that is easy to use. The clear signage helps patrons navigate the platforms and subway directions. The MTR network is fairly complex, with multiple routes coming into a single station, so knowing that a train will arrive every few minutes means I don't need to remember the schedule. At my destination, the process of following the signage and tagging off at the gate reverses.

When every component works well, passengers don't need to think about what contributed to such a seamless experience.

Princeton University psychologists found it only takes one-tenth of a second to form an impression of another person (Wargo, 2016). In the blink of an eye, we decide whether or not to trust. There is a similar effect on business operations. The customer experience is created through their interactions, or touchpoints, with the process and the team. Whether automated or manual, each touchpoint adds an extra layer of impression to the customer's experience.

Taking the train varies widely across countries and service providers. My train experiences in Italy, France, Germany, and Japan left very different impressions. The services provided reflected the management style and the cultures. When the schedule, people, and processes were not completely aligned to the customers' satisfaction, the service was hard to use, and it became easier to choose an alternative method of transport. The train passenger might opt to drive a car for convenience instead of navigating complex systems and schedules.

How well do your customers know what is going on behind the closed door of your operation? Some teams I have worked with wanted their customers to understand the effort and complexity that made the service happen. What customers see and experience is usually only the tip of the iceberg of business operations and processes. Just as I only saw the cleanliness and the ease of frequent MTR schedules in Hong Kong. From the point of sale to completion, service delivery involves hundreds, if not thousands, of people and at least a handful of systems.

A great customer experience is seamless. But customers don't need to understand the operation – it's only when things go wrong that they wonder what's happening in the background.

For products sold in the business-to-business wholesale market, the chances to interact with the consumers are limited. The product itself has to win the customers over. The number of sales and direct feedback provides insight into customer acceptance and satisfaction.

There are different ways to capture the Voice of the Customer. Satisfaction surveys help us understand how well customer-facing teams perform, and some even measure customer loyalty. The data is used to support the business decision-making process. A customer satisfaction score ranks the service experience through a series of questions. The score indicates how happy they are and how likely they are to recommend the products and services to others.

For example, a freight company might ask their customers to rank the speed of delivery service on a scale, with one being poor and ten being excellent. Specific, granular questions on individual process touchpoints will provide more quantitative data and insights.

Alternatively, a questionnaire of open questions captures customer feedback with more free flow text to express directly in the customer's own words. The beauty of such feedback is the richness of emotions and, at times, more detail of the customer's first-hand experience. However, it is time-consuming for a large-scale enterprise to manually go through masses of feedback comments. Using advanced technology can help to process the qualitative data.

Customer satisfaction and decision-making

Chances are the survey data only sits with the customer-facing department to support improvements in marketing, sales, and customer services operations. The high-level numbers are reported regularly, and some insights are shared. However, they might not be integrating the true essence of the responses into the strategic governance process, which can lead to missed commercial opportunities. The Voice of the Customer ends up sitting alone – waiting to be discovered and integrated.

Managing and analysing the data manually from multiple sources takes excessive time, effort, and capability in-house. Those customer satisfaction scores and feedback reported to board meetings only represent the surface of the deeper layers of the business operations. Most customer surveys are lengthy, with more than ten questions in a mix of multiple-choice and free answer text boxes. Lousy, repetitive questions lead to useless answers and scoring. Some people give up the survey halfway through as there's little to keep them interested. The result is poor completion rates.

A poorly designed survey means you end up only with extremely happy or dissatisfied insights into the customers' world. Ratings are equalised as an average score, so the executive board sees customer loyalty results, month-on-month, that don't reveal the customers' true feelings. It gives the governance team a false sense of comfort and potentially a wrong priority focus. In some cases, the comfort bubble bursts when enough customers turn to media or other public channels to express their frustration and dissatisfaction. The wake-up call comes as a complete contradiction to the mildly worded reports the board has seen over time.

These situations happen when customer satisfaction data, media channels, and operations data are analysed in isolation. With little change in the satisfaction numbers and blandly worded commentary in the report, the noise made by other parties in the business overtakes the Voice of the Customer. Many customer advocates instead focus on adding new ways to service customers and increase satisfaction with greater accessibility. We still find little attention given to the data from those channels once the implementation is complete.

With so many systems platforms, surveys, and feedback, merging and processing tens of thousands of lines accurately in spreadsheets and databases is a specialist skill in short supply in the employment market. Presenting insights effectively for decision-making is a challenge when there is too much focus on the technicality of the numbers and analytics to explain the underlying story. Some proactive enterprises spend excessive resources transforming their teams and purchasing expensive analytics software to manually connect and process the data sources differently.

Technologies are changing the way we access and process unstructured data. Streams of continuous data flow remove the need to manually export data from various sources in batches, causing a lag in reporting. There is no reason to schedule an alarm clock to export the data in batches and manually process them for the morning staff briefing. Connecting the data streams through API leads to fewer constraints in integrating platforms. That also means the data streams, once connected to an analytics platform, are consolidated in a single platform and are continuously available. With a real-time feedback alert, the team can be proactive with customer feedback before leaving the premises.

Gone are the days of analysts pulling their hair out while manually cleansing thousands of lines from databases to accurately process the data. By the time the data cleansing was done, the customer feedback information was already outdated. AI and machine learning technologies are now used in qualitative data analysis to remove the data cleansing workload and free up the team for more valuable tasks. Processing that took weeks of human effort now takes minutes.

Technologies used in performing thematic analysis identify patterns of meaning in unstructured written language by the customers themselves. It provides new insights on themes and keywords with quantitative measures of frequency of appearance in the customers' words (Medelyan, 2021).

By using technologies for thematic analysis on customer feedback, Greyhound Lines, an affordable long-distance travel provider in North America, reduced their analytics times tenfold. Technology showed a considerable volume of insights that the internal team would not have been able to find. These insights helped connect the commercial analytics team with the operations network to improve the process every day. The customer survey went from more than thirty questions that took a customer twenty minutes to complete, to five questions that took less than two minutes. This single change led to the survey completion rate jumping from 68 to 94 per cent. Asking different sets of questions outside of their norms revealed unknown insights. The technology has helped the Greyhound team increase their NPS score by twenty points (Thematic, 2018).

Analysing customer data and operational processes is like peeling layers off an onion. It is the best way to understand the true essence and root causes of feedback across the business. What does it mean when customers say they struggle to open an account online? Is it the website or the back-office process? Did the customers say the service was too pricey?

Is it really about the price, or are they dissatisfied with the value provided? Using these insights, the internal team can proactively identify the immediate process and actions that caused such an experience. Through operations process analysis, they can understand how to continually improve the process and add value to the customer experience.

In corporate governance, having transparency of the Voice of the Customer in a real-time visual brings meaningful information into the boardroom. Integrating real-time data for decision-making allows opportunities to shine through the light of customer insights. The Voice of the Customer is no longer alone when it finally connects as part of the greater business providing the business with greater clarity of the upcoming opportunity ahead.

Managing customer expectations

We live with many expectations. Waking up in the morning, we turn on the bathroom tap and expect water. We flick the switch on the kettle and expect it to boil. We take the bus, expecting it to follow the same route. We arrive at a café expecting coffee. We go about our lives expecting things to happen with services that meet our needs as users and consumers.

Similarly, customer expectations come in different forms. As users of city water systems, our expectations are not just about having water from the tap. We also want a well-maintained and sustainable water supply network. For a customer looking to purchase an electronic appliance, safety compliance, running costs, and user comfort can be essential factors in the buying decision. In public transport systems, the cost of the fare, the convenience of stops, and the frequency of services are close to the users' hearts. Café goers often choose the best tasting coffee, but the time it takes to get a takeaway on a busy morning can be the deciding factor.

Understanding customers' expectations and aligning them with operational processes helps enterprises consistently build and deliver value to their needs.

Case study: Fantastic Freight

Fantastic Freight has a call centre team of three hundred people, with one third based in head office and the rest outsourced in Asia.

A customer survey indicated frustration with the call waiting time on the customer service hotline. The satisfaction survey showed that customers who had spoken to the team were also more dissatisfied than in previous months.

The leaders looked at the call centre software to automatically optimise and reduce the waiting time by distributing the calls to the representatives available. But no further changes could be made. One team leader suggested making different technologies available to the customer through alternative channels – such as a web application and chat.

The leadership team decided it was a worthwhile potential solution to resolve the waiting time issue. A business case demonstrated the benefit of reducing waiting time and improving customer satisfaction by implementing the new technology as part of the call centre solutions. Further discussion with the technology vendor showed they could provide AI software as a robotic representative, as well as the basic web application. With the team excited about tapping into the latest technology, the idea was quickly incorporated into the business case as part of the solution.

Implementation of the solutions took additional effort and time, and it turned out that the customer knowledge base had not been regularly updated. The depots' processes and contacts were not current, and scanning data was stored in different operating systems. It was too difficult to integrate the systems, so the technology could not accurately answer simple questions. Customers ended up calling the same phone number to obtain an answer.

When the department conducted a stocktake with the team on how they helped the customer resolve the service issues, they recognised that technology could not replace the manual processes of communicating with various internal departments.

Upon completion of the implementation, the waiting time for the representatives had mildly improved, but customer satisfaction of the calls was still low. The team was disappointed to see the results of the satisfaction survey. With the customer satisfaction score as a key performance indicator for the organisation, the executive team started to look at why the numbers were still not improving.

They discovered that call centre individual performance measures had changed to the number and duration of calls taken in the month before the satisfaction score dropped. The performance framework indicated that shorter calls were more effective, so the team altered their behaviour to keep calls as short as possible to improve their performance. The troubleshooting baseline from internal data was about five minutes on the phone while the representative contacted various depots and departments.

The change of the contact centre team behaviour meant customer queries were not completely resolved during the first call, hence many issues developed into more significant concerns. When the customer had to call back a second time, they were far more dissatisfied with the call waiting time and the service. The second phone call took more than ten minutes, thus reducing the availability of the team members for initial calls.

This led to a review of the individual performance measuring framework for the call centre, and a refocus on how best to meet the customers' needs. Once they put those needs first, the team found a balance between customer satisfaction and performance. With additional effort in systems and processes change, the technologies were eventually able to provide more accurate information online and reduce the number of calls.

Quantifying customer expectations

Humans live with many defined structures, for example, our lives used to follow the sun, and now we follow the clock. And with those come expectations such as the number of hours we work, when we should eat, and how long we should sleep.

These social norms can impact the customer's expectations. Some might feel pressure to buy a new car or a new house. Or to express individuality through product choices. Those create particular needs and expectations of how services and products align with the customer's values. Moreover, their expectations vary depending on their personal experience with similar products, changing technologies, and market competition.

For example, appliance branding and the quality of other products under the same umbrella can create an expectation and unique value for customers. Some will opt for a brand that provides a lifetime guarantee, while others go for the lowest price. Understanding the customers you choose to service will help you meet their expectations.

Most, if not all, customer expectations can be translated into quantifiable and measurable quality requirements for the design, manufacturing, and delivery of services and products. In the Six Sigma methodology, we identify the essential qualities of the customer's voice through the Critical to Quality (CTQ) tree (Kubiak & Benbow, 2016).

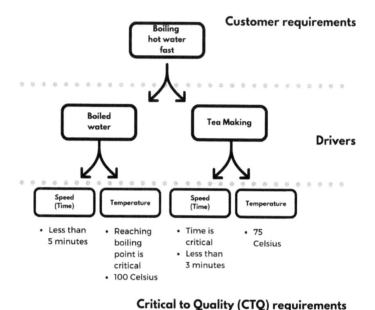

Customer requirements

Boiling
hot water
fast

Boiled
water

Tea Making

Drivers

| Speed (Time) | Temperature | Speed (Time) | Temperature |

- Less than
  5 minutes

- Reaching
  boiling
  point is
  critical
- 100 Celsius

- Time is
  critical
- Less than
  3 minutes

- 75
  Celsius

Critical to Quality (CTQ) requirements

Figure 7: Developing the Critical to Quality requirements tree

It is a simple diagram that places quantifiable requirements from the Voice of the Customer into an organised structure. The quality measurements become clear guidelines for making end products and services.

Case study: TangoBliss

TangoBliss is a household appliance brand whose target market is young households seeking quality products at affordable prices. The product development team is working to understand the customers' expectations of new-generation water kettles.

Electronic kettles are a standard appliance in the marketplace. The team knows their customers expect it to boil water reasonably fast, given that most households are busy. However, with the trend toward herbal and oriental tea, a water temperature of 100° Celsius is too hot. From the information gathered, the team has decided that time and water temperature are quantifiable measures of customer expectations. The team used these requirements to determine the technical specifications of the product.

While most kettles are similar in functionality, the materials and design can differentiate them from each other. The team has learned that their customer focus group cares about the sustainability of materials and implications for later disposal of the appliance.

Aligning the customer-facing team with operations

TangoBliss's manufacturing team worked alongside the product design team for several weeks. The new generation design comes with a range of settings in response to customer feedback. The kettle stops if the users press a button for tea instead of boiling water.

Before assembling the products, the manufacturing team went to a new product roadshow to learn how customers would use the new product. It gave the team a sense of appreciation and understanding of why the product was changing.

Assembling the newly designed kettle is more challenging than expected because the process includes additional fine components. The manual assembly process is also slower as it requires greater precision than other products.

The leader of the assembly production studies the best way to assemble new products and briefs the team on the risks of defects in the process. Together, they proactively reviewed the workstation setup for ease of assembly and to ensure the correct tools were available for the smaller components.

With understanding and support from the assembling operations, TangoBliss's new water kettle is on track for launch in the next quarter.

The story of TangoBliss's new product leading to a realignment of operations setup is not unusual in the industry. In most enterprises, the scale of change may differ depending on the product and service design. A product manager or owner should be the customer's internal advocate, overseeing the changes across the teams and ensuring all the moving parts are on track to deliver the expected quality.

Winning the last mile

New offerings and operational changes have become business-as-usual in a fast-paced, service-oriented enterprise.

While it is great for the business to adapt to changing market needs, it can feel like the daily routine is constantly disrupted if the team is not well-prepared. While the team wants to do well and care for the customers, change can be overwhelming.

A best practice strategy ensures the cross-functional team is on board with the customer's value proposition. The team will have renewed empathy for the customer and are more likely to be part of the solution if they put themselves in their customers' shoes. It would be helpful if some of the team were also customers, as they could provide a thorough and honest perspective of potential improvements to the product and service.

Setting up the product launch process and the logistical structure to support the different functional teams will help deliver the product to customer satisfaction. Using templates as a standard way of working in product operations can ensure the teams are aligned with the clarity of specifications in the communications. Service Level Agreements (SLA) within the internal departments provide the comfort of commitment and ensure timely delivery internally.

One such example is the final packaging that may include additional parts, such as cables, that need to be ordered through external parties by the procurement team. The timely delivery of procurement activities is crucial to the final packaging process and can impact the product launch timeline. Having clarity of service agreements between the internal functions provides peace of mind, helps both parties to prioritise the workload, and holds the shared responsibilities to a high standard.

> New offerings and operational changes have become business-as-usual in a fast-paced, service-oriented enterprise.

How are the parts and services structured in the enterprise resources planning (ERP) system to ensure easy accessibility? Are the product specifications and communications set up in the enterprise knowledge management system? Are the right stakeholders contributing their domain expertise to a successful launch? How would your customer-facing team communicate the order? What is the delivery target from the point of order?

The complexity involved in a product launch requires strong teamwork. The leadership team needs to advocate cooperation and embed those practices. This enables the enterprise to cater to the complexity of a changing operation and meet the customers' ever-expanding needs.

Don't jump the gun

Once you've engaged with the customers, there is a long wish-list of potential initiatives. The customer is excited, the team is ready to make changes, and the executive is keen to see action.

This is the time to be cautious and make decisions with a cool head.

Just when we think we have clarity about the Voice of the Customer, it dissolves as the team has to prioritise real needs based on the wish-list. Imagine having a wall of potential action points on Post-it notes or an almost endless spreadsheet from your customers. It would be fantastic to wave a magic wand and grant all their wishes, but this is rarely the case.

There can be a great benefit in inviting a panel of internal key stakeholders who are involved or impacted to participate in the decision-making process. Remember, the customers do not know the operations. Seemingly simple action points from the customer and the customer-facing team can have severe implications for the rest of the business processes. It is always good to involve upstream internal stakeholders when discussing potential changes.

Identifying the stakeholders' influence and interest will help the team advocate for customers' needs and identify common interests.

Five steps to innovation

It takes practical steps to translate new ideas into a viable trial to create a sustainable commercial opportunity.

Inspect

We inspect the customers' future vision and assess how it aligns with our internal strategy. We learn which activities and products are of interest and find out how they can better align with the shared new vision.

Assess

From our understanding of the activities, we assess the commercial value for the customers and the business. Comprehending the new value offered through solving a problem can help the team quantify the cost and benefit.

Formulate

We can start formulating the new offering and the related processes with the information on hand. There is more understanding of the processes and resources involved to build an estimated cost of service model. Knowing what the potential new offering means, we can engage the team to discuss how they can come on board and develop it further.

Decide

Innovation can be provided as a current service, an add-on or a new offering. There are usually more features on the wish list than we can include in the new offering, so it is time to decide the priority with the customers. The design of the trial offer should be informed by understanding how the offering is perceived by the market and its buying behaviour.

Evolve

With a small group of customers engaged, it is time to trial with a larger market to gather more data and validate the innovation. There need to be feedback channels to understand emerging market needs as the trial continues, as some innovative offerings may meet with mixed reactions. Understanding the success criteria is the key to delivering innovation that may disrupt the status quo in the market space and solve a problem for your customers.

Facilitate group consensus

The first step in streamlining the outcomes from customer ideation is removing duplication, then categorising themes in the action points to understand where improvements are needed.

Affinity grouping gets the participants to brainstorm and group the action points in terms of similarities; for example, feedback on changing the website's colour and improving the shopping cart checkout fall within the same technical function. The service design function supports input for enhancing the taste of food and serving size. Affinity grouping with mutual agreement by the participants simplifies and identifies the higher-level topics of interest at the functional level.

Remember, there is always a chance that some topics may evolve into much larger items through the discussion. Facilitation is important to ensure stakeholders understand the purpose of the exercise and stay on track when discussing the action points. A practical exercise involves setting a time limit for discussing each item. Ideally, scope the items in five to ten-minute discussions to get a general view from the group.

When the timer buzzes, the team can use the 'Fist of Five' hand gesture to express their readiness to move on to the next topic. It provides a quick, easy indicator to gauge feedback and group consensus. The gesture is fine for all personalities and is particularly helpful where people have different cultural and language backgrounds. I learned the 'Fist of Five' method in the early days of my Six Sigma training. Participants hold their hands up with a gesture to show the level of consensus they give on the topic in discussion.

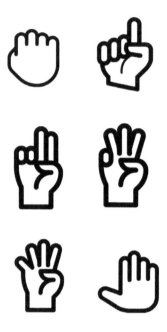

Figure 8: Fist of Five

A fist is a no-go, showing the person opposes the idea. They have significant concerns and need to be convinced before any further progress can be made on the consensus.

One finger (not the middle finger) indicates the participant has significant concerns but is willing to agree and move on.

Two says the participant is not happy with the idea but will accept the group decision.

Three fingers mean the participant is neutral but offers support.

Four fingers signal the participant is largely happy with the idea and agrees.

All five fingers show the participant thinks the idea under discussion is the best way forward and gives full support.

No one wants to be dragged into a conversation they are not interested in. If the discussions cannot finish within the allocated time, the topic can (with consensus) be parked until later. Review items in the parking lot at the end of the session or allocate them to a smaller group of interested people.

The wonderful thing about cross-functional stakeholder discussions is that the general consensus is clear, and the process for obtaining it is transparent. It removes the guesswork and reduces potential politics that arise from a lack of involvement in the decision-making process. The various parties and stakeholders participate as equal individuals, contributing their knowledge and tabling their needs.

It may not be easy to have all parties participating – that will depend on the team's history and willingness to work together. Hence the work of engagement in decision-making starts by individually connecting the stakeholders to warm them up to the idea of change. With built-in psychological safety support, different parties can share their needs and have their opinions heard. The intention is for individual engagement to build trust and understanding.

The facilitation process may seem lengthy, but it is still the fastest route to success. The actual group discussions, if facilitated well, are unlikely to take more than two or three working days. Individual conversations can be as simple as water cooler chats or a phone call to touch base. If the team is working and communicating closely, the facilitation will be easy with mutual understanding of the core of the topics that need to be discussed.

From consensus to action

The actions described above should narrow potential action points to become feasible. In the same setting, stakeholders can identify the group's priority using a multi-voting method. This involves each stakeholder having three to five votes to indicate their preferences. It is done knowing that each participant is a subject matter expert. Use it for data gathering to engage teams across the business and gauge buy-in from the start.

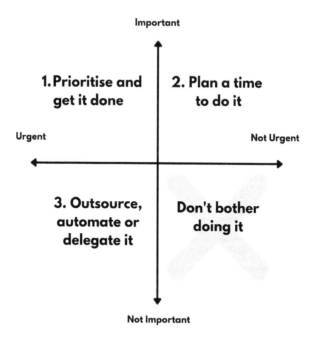

Figure 9: Eisenhower Decision Matrix

The Eisenhower Decision Matrix is the next tool to use with the emerging group of actions. Also known as Stephen Covey's four-quadrant model, this helps groups identify which actions are urgent and important. That's helpful when it turns out that all urgent actions are regarded as important, even though we know that's not the case. Those can be re-prioritised as Urgent but Not Important. Going through the action groups helps build a visual understanding of the groups' priorities and needs.

Not surprisingly, given the investment of time and effort, sponsoring executives expect groups to get into action. Intentional facilitation of group consensus opens up the conversation to the decision-making process to finalise the actions.

The decision path to action can be peculiar. At times, getting support for improvement ideas can feel like swimming across a river and figuring out ways to stay afloat. It comes down to identifying which actions can be resourced in the current capacity and the appetite to change.

The service team or product owner can gradually implement minor change requests within the level of operation delegation with the existing resources. New initiatives will need to represent significant value to compete with existing priorities and be actioned sooner.

Extensive changes, such as acquiring new technologies to provide a service, need more thought and usually a business case for additional resources. The business case and the justification go through several approval processes internally to obtain the necessary funding and resources.

For the best chance of success, it is smart to advocate for the customers' voice and mutual consensus from stakeholders in group discussions. The level of engagement and depth of knowledge built during group discussions generates greater confidence in the proposal – particularly for the financial executives. Risk management, along with the estimate of a positive return on investment and quantifiable data, helps justify the business case.

A sensible way of taking action is to allow the process of engagement and decision-making to take its course with intentional steering towards the business's best interests. Jumping into action without deliberate engagement or consensus can lead to risky outcomes and create new gaps in customer expectations. Speed of delivery and business risk is a constant tipping scale that needs to balance throughout the whole process. This is crucial for new service delivery as well as changing technologies in customer-facing areas.

Winning hearts by doing good

Businesses that do good by being socially responsible, being ethical and caring for the environment are closer to their customers' hearts. Like many others, I look out for goods and products that do good for myself and others. That includes caring for the safety and well-being of workers, minimising the impact on our environment and the subsequent implications for future generations.

A survey led by IBM found that 81 per cent of respondents identified as either value-driven or purpose-driven consumers who look for products and services aligned with their values.

Fifty-seven per cent of respondents were willing to change their buying behaviours to reduce negative environmental impact (Haller et al., 2020).

Similarly, PwC Consumer Insights Survey found that 50 per cent of the global survey participants are becoming more eco-friendly. Their survey also reported that an average of 80 per cent of consumers in Southeast Asia and 67.5 per cent of consumers in the Middle East reported being significantly more environmentally conscious (PricewaterhouseCoopers, 2021). With an economic outlook of 5.7 per cent growth projection in 2022 and projected growth of more than 6 per cent in Asia by the International Monetary Fund (IMF), it is increasingly important to identify changing consumer preferences in the global regions (International Monetary Fund, 2021).

The change in digital technologies, health restrictions, and remote working helped accelerate the consumers' purchasing behaviour change in recent times. To be resilient, both consumers and businesses have to pivot and adopt new ways to meet changing demand.

With a shift of consumer and customer preferences, businesses need to focus not only on profit, but also on people and the planet (Elkington, 2018). Adapting the new thinking means the business and operation are likely to be closely aligned with the values shared with the customers.

These are the steps that shift business to doing good:

Commit to the vision

Customers are watching closely to see whether businesses that share their vision are actually committing to them. The ongoing commitment is an important action that speaks louder than the words on annual reports and presentations at AGMs.

Questions to ask:

What would a genuine commitment to the vision look like?

Does it lead to any change in the governance setup?

Identify shared values

Every business has its own set of core values, and it is wise to review them regularly. While it is good to keep essential core values and beliefs, it is also important to assess how they align with the customers' values.

Questions to ask:

Who are your ideal customers?

What values do your customers share that you love?

Change your practice

Engage teams to work toward shared values with your most aligned customers. This means looking at the activities across the board to assess if the practice aligns with the values.

If courage is an important value shared, identify activities in the day-to-day business practice that reflect it. Fostering a culture of courageous creativity in business and taking a stand to improve safety standards are courageous actions.

Questions to ask:

Which activities do not align with your values?

What can you do to change them?

Measure progress

Knowing the ongoing progress and achievements made toward a shared alignment will motivate the team and excite your customers. Progress measurement needs to be authentic and meaningful when meeting value alignment.

Questions to ask:

How do we measure progress?

What makes the measurement meaningful?

Engage with successes

Despite having limited time, customers read the fine print of products they purchase and often independently research online to determine if the product ingredients and production process align with their values. It makes sense to share the work in progress and successes to make it easier to support their research and provide accurate information in the communication channels.

Questions to ask:

Which platforms are the best to share the progress and successes?

How should they be presented to encourage more engagement?

The constraints of production and existing infrastructure mean it can be a bold move for some manufacturing and logistics businesses to conduct this exercise. Early adopters willing to take the first steps will be rewarded with their customers' love and sustainable long-term growth.

PART THREE

THE VOICE OF
THE EMPLOYEE

People are the key to the business. In this part of the book, we'll examine the true voice of the employee for consistency in governance and smoother implementation of strategy across the enterprise.

People eat strategy

'Culture eats strategy for breakfast'

– Peter Ducker

Let's be frank. When a company puts their strategy out as if it was an all-you-can-eat free buffet, staff will take any piece they like and do whatever they want with it.

Can you think of a time when you have worked on or come across a strategy? Many are worked out in some remote boardroom, appear in fancy presentations, and are never seen again. Or strategic initiatives are sent to the executive office to be implemented across the organisation. The strategic work programme is on top of everything else the team already has to do.

This and other similar cases of poorly managed strategy creation and planning open the door to the buffet. How do we nurture the strategy to fruition instead of being eaten up and vanishing for good?

Enterprise strategy and structure

The vision and strategy are the steering mechanism for the sustainable competitive future of a business. Technology and disruption of business models challenge traditional, infrastructure-heavy enterprises to remain competitive.

A vision is an aspiration, mental image, and desired outcomes. An existing logistics business might want to expand its network, obtain market share, and be the industry leader. A manufacturing business may have the foresight to drive social and environmental sustainability through its products. Those desires formulate a vision of the future for the enterprise and inform its strategy.

Once a vision is created, we need a way to make it happen. That is when strategy planning kicks in. Understanding the desired future makes it possible to formulate the plan and actions to progress toward the outcomes.

In a logistics network, the vision to expand can turn into a strategy to acquire more assets in a new location or different means of transportation to reach an under-served population. For a manufacturer to be socially and environmentally sustainable, the strategy could involve only working with certain accredited suppliers and adopting environmentally friendly practices.

The strategy gives the wider leadership team direction to meet and support the vision. An enterprise structure is shaped to support the strategy. Details of responsibility should be clearly outlined in the structure, which comes with allocating resources to progress toward the strategic direction and execution.

The enterprise structure can take many different forms. Traditionally it was hierarchical with centralised authority and top-down leadership. This industrial approach to manufacturing produced large volumes of standardised products in factories after the world wars.

We can see this in two examples.

Bob is a supply chain manager who reports directly to the head of supply chains. Bob's workload, including any additional tasks, is delegated by his manager to ensure alignment with the team and the organisation's needs. Bob's manager reports to a one-up manager and through many layers of linear reporting to the chief executive. They need approval from the manager above at each level before taking action.

Times changed as the economy became more project-oriented, with enterprises adopting a slightly less centralised model with a cross-functional focus. This led to a matrix organisation with dual or multiple managers responsible and accountable for a shared unit of people resources.

Some enterprises might take it further into a network matrix where someone could report to multiple managers on allocated work.

Mary is a team leader for a logistics company. Her direct manager is the operations manager, and her other reporting line goes to the project management office manager in head office for a project she is responsible for. She might also be responsible for health and safety change implementation, with a reporting line to the national health and safety manager. Effectively, she reports directly to one manager and the other two managers for special projects.

CHRISTINE W.K. YIP

Another form of enterprise structure is a decentralised network of tribes that have emerged with the implementation of the Agile way of working. Each tribe holds a core function supporting the enterprise strategy and is organised into a chapter. Think of it as a book chapter with subsections. They are related, but individual chapters serve different messages. In organisational terms, the chapter is a flattened hierarchy with two to four tribes and only two or three layers to the top executive. In comparison, the old-fashioned centralised, hierarchical structure can have anything from a handful to more than ten reporting managers in a single linear line from the frontline to the top executive.

The changes to organisational structures over time are summarised in the table below.

Past decade	Present decade	Future possibilities
Centralised hierarchical organisation structure	A combination of hierarchical matrix and network structure	Decentralised network of tribes
Manufacturing standards to produce quality goods	Value-driven priorities to create quality services	Data-driven approach to create innovative digital services
Forced to stick to the schedule	Rapid change of schedule requires agility	Everything is available on demand
Technology-centric implementation	Human-centric implementation	Blended human-robotic implementation
Expensive technology	People are expensive	Little or no uptake of low-value work
Less diversity in workers and management team	Diversity of a team is inevitable due to generational changes (Fry, 2020)	Blended workforce of humans and machines as a team.

Table 1: Changes to organisational structures

Roles and responsibilities

Although the strategy and structure are set to go, negotiation for ad hoc changes can still happen. Strategy and planning require sponsorship and coordination to stay intact; otherwise, the structure will likely go in all directions and crash and burn the strategy.

One of the worst offenders is the lack of clarity of roles and responsibilities in the structure. This sees roles modified by the team in day-to-day operations without fully aligning with the original intent.

Enterprise operation is a complicated beast. It takes the largest share of resources to run and keep things in check across the business. The team members might have a different view of which strategy might work with their perception of history and understanding of the business. Without engaging the team, the organisational structure can appear intact on paper. However, the core value and intent are eroded if people are unwilling to align their activities to the new strategy.

A misinformed perception can fuel actions to protect the business operation. However, good intentions can cause poor judgment and activities that damage the business.

Alignment of the strategy and processes ownership is necessary to prevent disconnection of the strategy, structure, and people's roles. People can take some ownership in the new strategy and the process to constructively and consistently shape outcomes.

Process accountability

Implementing any new strategy requires support. As an organisation, process accountability is critical to migrating the status quo to the new strategy.

Case Study: Honey Bear Foods

Honey Bear Foods has recently gone through a strategic review of its business vision to focus on online business growth. As the company has been purely a food manufacturer and exporter, this results in changes in the business structure with additional resources to boost the online channels and distribution with less focus on manufacturing operations.

The team is excited about the vision but has reservations about what will happen to their roles and future in the operational areas. Seeing resources reducing in their area as the business reallocates staffing to the online branding and presence also means the team has to work harder to deliver the same outcome with fewer staff. That brings another level of discomfort.

The online channel for Honey Bear Foods is still in the early stages of development. But the large volume of online orders has impacted the usually stable manual manufacturing operations. This has added fuel to the team's speculation that the online business will ruin their good performance and affect their bottom-line performance. Morale on the manufacturing floor is gradually lowering because of tension between the old and the new.

The new team is frustrated by the lack of support and guidance from the manufacturing operations of the product development and logistics processes. In the technology design, no document could guide them to the critical touchpoints to help improve the experience for online customers and the internal operations. The performance of the online business initiative starts to take a hit.

With all indicators looking increasingly pear-shaped, the leadership team urgently needs to find ways to get the business back on track.

The story of Honey Bear Foods is not uncommon. Throughout the business and people changeover, the team focuses solely on the day-to-day manual manufacturing operations, with no focus on the enterprise processes. Gradually, the business operations build inside people's heads with multiple, parallel versions of the realities. It becomes difficult to retain good operational performance while creating new business opportunities without clear ownership of the process and shared accountability in the new strategy.

Honey Bear Foods (and others in similar situations) needs a high-level stocktake on the status quo enterprise processes before the new strategy kicks in. A snapshot of current enterprise processes will give the executives an indication of where the gaps are and which team can support the change in advance. Change management support is needed to help engage the individuals to work as a team to resolve issues during the transition to the new direction.

Process accountability shared as a team will develop problem-solving capability, creating new solutions and ensuring they work with the different process streams across the organisation. This results in greater individual and team ownership, increasing the ability to improve the checks and balances on performance across the enterprise.

HR data on process

When we mention human resource data, we likely think of annual leave, people's performance, and productivity. But there is a significant gap in the data on people's capacity to lead and perform process ownership, problem-solving ability, and performance in implementing the strategy.

People can make or break the business – even more so if the company is highly dependent on manual processes to solve problems and deliver products and services to its customers.

While technologies are used to monitor systems and measure the success of individual business processes, problem-solving performance is hard to measure. However, consolidating reliable data such as project performance, operations process performance, and team feedback forms a constructive method for measuring soft skills. The consolidated data set can be used in understanding the team's capabilities and ability to implement changes as an ongoing measure.

Powerful team

Vision and purpose

A vision can also be a mission if it is important enough. For example, it would be challenging for some industries to be the first service provider to achieve zero waste in the supply chain. Virgin Atlantic's vision statement is to be the most loved travel company (Virgin Atlantic, 2019). For a business, the vision is a starting point for fostering a sense of purpose in the team, even if it is strictly commercial.

Not every individual is explicitly aware of their vision for their life; some live day-to-day without the resources to look too far ahead. That's why it can be difficult for a team to understand the business vision if it is not relevant to them. For those who want to contribute to the organisation's success, not understanding the purpose can be daunting while working long hours on repetitive tasks. The disconnection of vision disengages the team. Connecting the business vision with the team creates a sense of belonging. When you add structural clarity into the mix, it is clear who owns the 'how' in supporting the vision and the strategy.

Simon Sinek's Golden Circle theory suggests that too few organisations know their 'why' or the purpose of their existence. And he thinks only some know the 'how' – the logistics of business success. But most organisations know 'what' they do. Sinek also believes that too few leaders choose to inspire with value and purpose (Sinek, 2011).

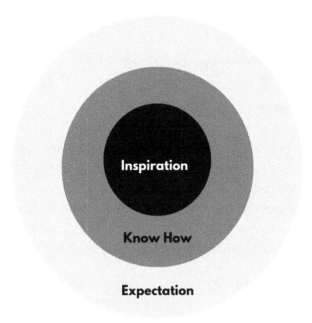

Strategy Implementation Circle

Figure 10: Strategy implementation circle

When enterprises introduce new strategies, it's common to see a timeline demonstrating expectations of what will be achieved. There's very little on the 'how', and the inspiration is largely business talk that hardly enthuses the team. While it is useful for the team to know that the business objectives are shifting, people are left to fill in the blanks of achieving the expectations without feeling like they are on board with the reasons for change.

If the reason for change does not inspire the team, there will be little motivation to figure out the 'how' and deliver on expectations. Strategy implementation can be sluggish when expectations are unmet.

Understanding motivation

I have a Siamese cat and have come to realise that the single purpose of a cat is to survive on its own terms. No doubt it is a lovely pet, and we have connected as a family, but the cat doesn't turn up unless he has a need. Most animals don't do more than necessary if they are satisfied with their immediate needs. It reminds me of a Bible verse, 'Look at the birds in the sky: They do not sow, or reap, or gather into barns, yet your heavenly Father feeds them' (Matthew 6:25-34).

The difference between humans and animals is that we think beyond the present. If we were animals, we would go with whatever our environment throws at us – and be fine with it. But we are not. It is a gift that we can work beyond the now and think into the future.

When it comes to exploring our future, we are likely to ask specific questions. Why are we doing what we are doing now? Will we be doing the same thing in the future? Is it a good thing to do? How is it going to benefit me?

It is natural and reasonable to consider our desires and needs before others'. Maslow's hierarchy of needs is a timeless description of the various levels of human needs. According to Maslow, at the most basic level, we must have our physiological needs of food, shelter, and warmth to survive. As those needs are met, we are more likely to explore love, belonging, self-fulfilment, and contribute to a cause for a wider group through our actions (Maslow, 1943).

Maslow's Hierarchy of Needs

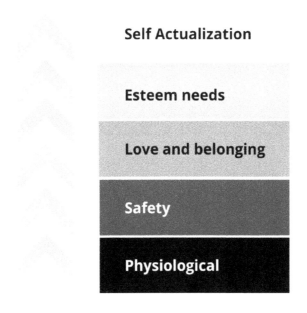

Figure 11: Maslow's Hierarchy of Needs

Personality type can also impact motivation. The Myers-Briggs Type Indicator groups identify inward and outward, thinking or feeling, perception or judgment, subjective or objective, individual or team-oriented personalities. In each category, an individual can share a blend of the two spectrums and learn to be aware of their personal preference for a job (Myers, 1962).

Similarly, psychologist Anne Ellis has suggested that people are generally motivated by categories such as autonomy and freedom, creation and pursuit of ideas, security and stability, success and results, changing environment, financial incentives, competition and team support (Ellis, 2020). Various personality profiling tools help team members understand their personal values, beliefs, and preferences at work. Personal connection is the key ingredient for strong teamwork, so using these tools help managers and teams get to know each other better.

The demographic and personality difference of the workforce leads to a mix of needs and values appearing in the workplace. A baby boomer, a middle-aged mother working full time, and a young digital native have different worldviews, values, and needs. The differences in their understanding and perceptions of the world impact their day-to-day decisions at home and work.

Despite the differences in backgrounds, connecting personally by knowing each other through shared interests at the workplace can foster inter-generational teamwork. Sometimes it's surprising to find how aligned we are despite our differences. When working on digitalising network performance testing for a logistics company, the most supportive people I met on the shop floor and in middle management were older males who had been waiting for automation and more accuracy in the testing process for the network for years. I went from being a single person pushing the business case to the senior board, to having personal support directly from them and their peers in the organisation. Teamwork helped shape the business case and brought it across the line for funding and implementation.

The profile of a team comes from observing and understanding the demographic and personalities. The team profile provides another perspective and insight into the shared values of the group and their motivation drivers. A good match of the value of the team aligning with the strategic purpose brings powerful teamwork as a competitive advantage. In a larger enterprise, our workforce comprises people from all walks of life. Therefore, it is helpful to use constructive methods to gather objective workforce data and uncover ways to ignite the team to be personally onboard with the purpose of work.

Cultivating a creative team

Competitive advantages come from the ability to create and iterate. If a team is fixated on only doing what and when they are told, the heavy burden of figuring out how to deliver and run the operations falls on the few rather than the many. To avoid this, we need to cultivate teams with a shared purpose and a creative mindset for long-term success.

Carol Dweck, the psychologist who studies growth mindset, found that employees are 34 per cent more likely to feel a strong sense of ownership in companies that embrace challenges and continuous learning (Levine, 2019). By understanding the motivations behind the workforce, it is possible to foster a learning environment of ownership and creativity.

Think of a five-year-old girl drawing a picture. She draws with colour pencils, available paper, and there is plenty of time to draw. Given no boundaries, she can draw whatever she likes using her imagination and creativity.

Strategy implementation is like requesting a drawing. Even with some form of instruction, how the picture looks depends entirely on the team and the individuals involved. The delegation of authority and trust are critical elements to enable creative thinking and problem-solving. With clarity of responsibility and roles, individuals can independently take ownership to solve problems and contribute to the larger strategic picture.

Part of being creative is removing boundaries and red tape. This can be done by temporarily removing them in a designated setting, such as a company-wide, online innovation forum, a team-building exercise, or innovation retreat. That means while the team specialises in their day job, they have a way to contribute creativity as members of the wider organisation. If the platform is well-facilitated, groups with shared interests can learn from each other's insights, work to solve a complex problem and develop ideas on potential solutions for trial.

Group creativity can be unleashed through intentional facilitation processes. One of the most valuable techniques I have used is the Six Thinking Hats theory by Edward de Bono, the father of lateral thinking (De Bono, 1985). The idea is to have a range of functions and perspectives as a hat to put on yourself as you consider the topic. The colour of the hat dictates the way of thinking; for example, yellow for optimism, black for risk, and red for feeling and intuition.

Facilitating the group through a process can avoid groupthink. This happens when members become too familiar with each other and do not want to challenge or share a different opinion. In particular, if they have been working in a company culture with little psychological safety, to talk about different perspectives.

A process such as the Six Thinking Hats permits the team to be bolder in expressing themselves and helps break the behavioural habit in communications. Emerging creativity comes from rich and diverse discussions – not the other way around.

Case study: Flying High Aviation

Flying High Aviation is looking to improve its on-time performance for flight departures. The general manager of performance has gathered diverse employees to creatively explore the root causes and possible solutions for a trial. As it happens, the demand for new passenger flights has increased significantly as the market warms up to international travel. There needs to be a practical solution at speed to resolve the on-time performance issue.

The teams come from various parts of the airline and have a substantial understanding of the network's operation. The group started by throwing in what they knew from their area of expertise.

The customer advocate provided insights into customer experience, feedback, and complaint data to identify an area that is most likely to contribute to the on-time performance issue of the flights. So did the aviation network scheduling experts, operational leaders, third party suppliers, and the pilot who represented his peers in the conversation. The same concerns were raised again as they discussed performance.

The conversation grew into a huge number of issues and hundreds of potential areas for examination, given the complex nature of the topic. There did not seem to be any particular direction the group could take to the next level. A participant observed that it was partly because the participants were still largely sticking to their habitual thinking and using logic in their subject matter expertise.

A suggestion was made to consolidate the current ideas in discussion and explore key themes using the method. After an initial consolidation, a few topics of interest emerged. This included maintenance issues, scheduling requirements, and customer expectations.

By going through a theme using the Six Thinking Hats, the participants can constructively contribute to the topic through a different lens. The group makes progress towards a potential solution for a trial outside the domain of the maintenance team. The maintenance team feels supported as the conversation shifts from finger-pointing to collaborative brainstorming with the wider group's understanding.

Finally, the group generated a potential solution and were given a small trial to test its effectiveness. They found that better maintenance work scheduling can reduce the chances of last-minute aircraft replacement – one of the key reasons for late departure.

Building adaptivity

Times have changed. Enterprises used to lean on a handful of leaders, and the hierarchy of command flowed to the next level like a champagne tower. But a champagne tower with no agility and the domino effect of a broken glass at the bottom can be spectacularly unwelcome.

For an operation to be sustainable in our increasingly volatile world, having a structure with built-in agility and resilience can safeguard it from ongoing disruption.

Instead of having command flowing through the precious few, a more agile and resilient leadership operation can look like Japanese origami, the art of paper folding into shapes and figures. It was largely used for decorative purposes until its technical application was found to be useful in architectural and space technology design.

With several pieces of paper folded into shapes and supporting the whole, the shape is scalable and changeable by design. Each piece of paper supports the whole and shares the weight as it bounces around.

Even basic origami skills can create a variety of shapes and structures. The structure can be versatile depending on the needs and thinking at the time. Changing from a tower to a different shape is done by simply swapping the pieces around.

The beauty of origami is that you can use paper, a serviette, or even a sheet of metal to create a shape. Different materials bring different qualities to the structure.

If everyone is a piece of material in an origami organisation, the leaders perform an important function in building an autonomous group of strength and creativity. Given the number of people involved, connectivity and support mean they share the weight of the responsibility. When the chain of command is flat, the responsibility is shared, and decisions are made through smaller groups. Adopting an origami-style of organisation brings resilience.

Building a community of innovative leaders

Toyota Production System is a world-famous manufacturing system on lean, productivity, and quality improvement, but little is known about the intent to develop innovative leadership.

Kiichiro Toyoda, the founder of Toyota, originally started as a textile manufacturer. He envisioned building a fully Japanese-made car and 'catching up with America' in car manufacturing. That vision drove the family business to find a way to design and manufacture vehicles in Japan from scratch in the 1930s (Toyota Motor Corporation, 2012). At the time, cars were manufactured in Europe or America and imported into Japan for assembling.

Toyoda's vision led to the creation of a local supply chain. He knew that once the challenge of building the supply chain had started, the cost of parts and production must come down for the end products to be accepted by the consumers as affordable, privately owned transportation.

With limited resources, fulfilling the vision required a thinking team that shared the vision and could create new solutions independently. A team that would dare to identify areas of improvement from the status quo, come up with new ideas, and make sound judgments on the viability of potential solutions. Once a solution was identified, they were tasked to implement and sustain it as their own – until another improvement was identified and newer solutions implemented.

And so, the Toyota Production System was born.

Innovation starts with observation. The team had time to watch others completing production tasks over days or weeks. Whether the job was big or small, the ultimate goal was to identify where things could be improved and generate ideas. In today's manufacturing operations, where the focus is on optimising every minute of the people's hours, the value of intentional observation of the status quo is often underestimated. It is a crucial step to independent fact-gathering and critical thinking processes.

Unlike today where pre-made parts and technologies are readily available, the start-up Toyota had no luxury to design or purchase machinery to drive improvement. The leaders even discouraged purchasing external machinery as an improvement solution because it was seen as 'outsourcing the thinking', thus taking away chances for the team to go through the ideas development process.

The production system educated the team on the quality of their output and thinking systematically. The Andon traffic light system gave any team member authority to stop production if there was a defect on the line. Once stopped, the leader would go through the problem-solving process until the root cause was found. When the quality issue was resolved, production could resume with a green light for this line and the subsequent processes (Noji, 2019). While this was effective in eliminating defects from the manufacturing process, it was also an educational opportunity for the team to take ownership of problem-solving and implement a solution to enable the product to continue.

These are a few examples of how the Toyota Production System builds innovative leaders from a shared vision, creating standard norms for the team to be thinkers and idea creators. A strong sense of ownership to solve problems arises through those activities and facilitates a culture to continue reinventing itself.

Continuous invention from a community of innovative leaders enabled the company to grow from an impossible vision of building locally made cars to becoming a global corporation.

Understanding diversity

People make up the workforce, and their differences can change team dynamics, with differences in demographic makeup and cultural background impacting performance, productivity, and sustainability.

The manufacturing and logistics workforce has always been diverse. It is not uncommon to have team members on the shop floor whose ages range from eighteen to seventy. Different life stages, values, biological needs, and lifestyle desires affect how various demographic groups work.

Many baby boomers in the workforce are likely to retire or semi-retire in the coming years, which means gaps will need filling. This is particularly severe in the transport sector, which has already faced a shortage of truck drivers over recent decades. The American Trucking Association reports that the average age of the over-the-road truckload industry is forty-eight (ATA, 2019). Similar shortages of transport drivers have been reported in the United Kingdom, Australia, and New

Zealand. A survey conducted by the International Road and Transport Union with eight hundred road transport companies across twenty countries showed that 20 per cent of driver positions were unfilled in Eurasia. This is largely due to the industry's heavy reliance on experienced, qualified male drivers (IRU, 2021).

The pressure of filling the gaps doesn't stop here. With a lower birth rate, the OECD has projected a shrinking workforce across the globe. Specifically, there are likely to be twenty-five million fewer working-age people in Japan, twelve million in Germany, and three hundred million in China (Rouzet et al., 2019). With a smaller working population pool and a perception of the unattractiveness of manufacturing and logistics industries, businesses need to look at ways to diversify their recruitment tactics to enable more female and younger people to be part of the workforce and train up unskilled workers.

Other than the aging population, our cultures are becoming more diverse despite being in the same country. By cultural differences, I mean personal values, beliefs, and ways of living that are different from others, whether race, gender identity, religious beliefs, economic and social status, or equality.

The perception and misunderstanding of different groups impact team dynamics and productivity. As a general perception, older team members have more years of experience in the business and can be a real asset. The younger generation of digital natives brings renewed perspective to an existing workplace.

But those perceptions are not always accurate. Getting to know the team personally to understand their contributions can change some impressions. Intentional facilitation to encourage the constructive expression of different opinions can help individuals feel valued, foster a sense of belonging, and support the team to be more creative in their thinking.

In the world of logistics and manufacturing, where most tasks are still manual, generational changes and cultural differences play a role in building effective teamwork. Perceptions form opinions and judgment. It is particularly important to remove biases regarding recruitment, recognition, and the continuous building of organisational culture.

Facilitating teamwork with the enterprise's value and purpose will channel energy into the right actions and help put aside individual differences.

Same yet different

The Asia Pacific (APAC) is a vibrant and extremely diverse region on the world map, with a GDP of USD26.99 trillion as of 2019 (The World Bank, 2021). The OECD projected that most Asia and Pacific countries will rebound in 2022 to pre-pandemic GDP with a higher growth projection than the rest of the world (OECD, 2021). Being relatively resilient in crises, it is a region with significant potential for growth and is a key location for many innovative manufacturers (The World Bank, 2021). It presents a unique opportunity to grow the talent pool to strengthen operations, seeing them stepping into future leadership roles and growing with the organisation.

Asia and Pacific countries are distinct from the rest of the globe in many ways.

Legal and regulations standards

Despite the number of countries involved in the European region, most follow European standards as part of the European Union. This is similar to Commonwealth countries and the United States. The shared understanding across the region makes it easier to navigate and implement global standards and policy.

However, the Asia Pacific and other emerging regions hold individual country regulations and standards with perspectives of philosophy, power, and authority that are different from the Western world and their neighbouring nations. Some countries are very restricted and authoritarian, while others are more transparent and democratic. The differences in the philosophy of the legal systems impact how the legislation is shaped and presented for enforcement, thus impacting internal management processes across the region. This perspective is likely to flow through to the management of organisations and how teams work together.

One example is the differences in employment legislation and the relationship with health and safety legislation, where enforcement of regulations varies from country to country. Local understanding of standards underpins the outcomes and requires strong engagement to navigate a balanced view of management processes in each country.

Cultural connection and understanding

People's life experience shapes their identity. We acquire new identities throughout our lives with events such as graduating from a particular university or becoming a parent.

Cultural heritage and their connection with others who share similarities form a huge part of our identity.

Alongside music, food is a known cultural connector – and particularly so in Asia. Common food items like red beans and taro are known as dessert flavours in Asia, and the shared understanding from this connection of interest and personal memories creates a special bond between individuals.

Another example is that the love of cooking meat on the bone in the Pacific cultures is similar to many Asian cultures. At the beginning of my New Zealand cultural journey, I found the Māori 'boil up' dish made with pork bone, watercress or puha (sow thistle), greatly resembles the Chinese style soup I grew up with.

The cultural connection of food goes deeper than surface knowledge or interests. It indicates a shared heritage, a likeness of choice that differentiates who we think are similar to us and how we connect with others. Consider how food can play a role in gluing the team across different nations and cultures to foster better teamwork.

The perspective of creativity

There are two opposing spectrums of acceptance in creativity amongst the Asian and Pacific cultures. While many cultures endorse creativity in arts and music, the perception of standing out from the crowd is not encouraged. Being creative means thinking differently and may lead to doing things outside of the cultural norms.

From a collective cultural perspective, it is generally more acceptable to be similar to others in the Asian and Pacific cultures in our behaviours. In particular, some Asian cultures have a strong preference for avoiding inconvenience to others by being different. If there is a need to be different, there is a strong preference to seek approval from the people seen as authority figures before even expressing the idea.

In workplaces, creativity can be perceived as deliberately working differently from the old ways. This may be seen as disrespectful to those with more experience in the area and the rules. Some cultures that suffer from limited resources encourage working outside the box to deliver solutions, but these might not align with management's perspective of quality standards.

Encouraging the team to adapt to new perspectives of balancing creativity and quality can be challenging. Hence the facilitation of change should be sensitive and respectful towards cultural differences, providing practical steps for the team to adopt more balanced creativity in cross-cultural teamwork across the region.

Develop a skill matrix and leadership pathway

In industries that rely heavily on people processes with the pressure of lower margins, staff retention and engagement are essential to keep the business operation running smoothly. A career path will ensure employees are growing and developing with the business. This can be achieved by deliberately creating a skill matrix with a clear enterprise strategy, structure, and functional roles to carve out the team's leadership pathways.

Building such a matrix means drawing out the common core competencies to be developed over time. These fulfil the needs of the workforce requirements now and in the future.

Any decision about which skills to include in the matrix is highly dependent on the type of business. For example, a transportation business requires systematic thinking and problem-solving skills, given that a single change in the operation can flow on to the next scheduled fleet departure. A service-oriented operation may focus on customer service and time management skills. The key is knowing which skills to prioritise for the team to develop over time, complement individual career advancement, and support business growth.

Choosing what to include in the skills matrix needs to be mutually agreed upon with the management team. In developing it, the management team needs both short and long-term views of performance sustainability and building a workforce with a somewhat uncertain strategic future. The matrix may vary slightly based on the functions and leadership pathways but should not be developed in isolation.

Once you are clear about the skills matrix, the next step is to develop leadership pathways. These inspire the team members to consider potential advancement options and guide management on ways to grow the capability in alignment with the operation's needs.

The skills matrix and leadership pathway are not static documents to file away. The key to this process is to regularly review against current needs and adjust the prioritisation of skills and future leadership requirements. Although core competencies are likely to remain the same, the external change of environment can mean some skills are more critical than others. For example, organisational resilience may become a greater focus as the team navigates challenging times. That means skills such as dealing with ambiguity and emotional intelligence can have higher priorities.

Regularly reviewing the skills matrix and leadership pathway helps strengthen the team by knowing and considering the needs of the time, keeping the enterprise energised with teams that have relevant skillsets, and sustainably growing the leadership.

Decision-making process

We make decisions every day, considering our options and choosing solutions that lead to what we want to achieve.

Research from Cornell University estimated that the average person makes 226.7 decisions per day on food alone (Wansink & Sobal, 2007). We obviously make more decisions than we thought. How conscious are the decisions made when we don't realise we are making them? What is the process? In the daily food decision example, are the food choices only to satisfy our physiological needs? Do thoughts of long-term lifestyle and health impact food decisions? Or are decisions sometimes made solely on deliciousness?

Similarly, when it comes to decision-making in business and operations, there is usually a pattern on who and how things are decided. That pattern may have become so familiar that we no longer need to consider the options before making a call.

Daniel Kahneman's book *Thinking, Fast and Slow* describes two thinking systems. System 1 is the fast, immediate, automatic, unconscious type of thinking and System 2 is the slow, logical, thoughtful calculation and conscious thinking process (Kahneman, 2013).

Delivery schedules heavily restrict manufacturing, transportation and logistics sectors, and are a major influence on decisions. A fear of delay can trigger an immediate decision to get the goods out the door rather than resolving the actual problems. This decision came through System 1, fast thinking. Another restriction is the level of authority implicit in a traditional hierarchical approval structure, where management controls the moving parts of the operation. This can trigger the team to wait for approval instead of problem-solving when an incident happens. It's another example of using System 1 fast thinking to react to the situation. Similar restrictions can be at play interchangeably and in isolation. That is firefighting.

Too much firefighting means slow, logical, and creative problem-solving thinking may not have a chance to kick in because of habitual, unconscious patterns that use fast thinking. It is worth noting that System 2 (slow, logical thinking and problem-solving) should be intentionally facilitated with time and resources. This will foster a problem-solving culture in any challenging and fast-paced business.

When it comes to enterprise decision-making, the traditional model can be summed up at three levels: operational, tactical, and strategic.

The first level involves day-to-day operations where the frontline team manages their allocated workload within the schedule and roster.

The second level is the tactical coordination of functions. This includes cross-functional decisions to ensure resources and materials are effectively allocated and managed to the operations.

The third level is strategy, where the vision and future direction of the enterprise is decided to ensure it remains competitive and sustainable.

Each level is responsible for its thinking and decisions via a vertical feedback loop. Vertical decision-making leads to a lack of transparency and is slow to respond to the needs of the operational team because decisions must go through so many layers of authority.

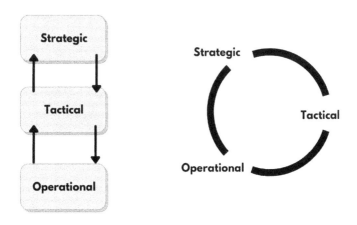

Figure 12: Vertical and multi-directional decision-making

With changes to a more agile, network organisational structure, the levels are more even as the teams share responsibilities. Multi-directional feedback loops mean all parties can contribute to the strategic, tactical, and operational decision-making process. They reduce the waiting time for decisions and generate more inclusive information and opinions.

Welcoming challenges

The word *challenge* shares similarities with an Asian fruit, the durian. For those who don't know, durian (the king of fruits) has a distinctively strong fragrance and flavour. You either love or hate it.

In the same way, challenges either scare or excite people. For those who love a challenge, it is an exciting prospect of adventure, the possibility of breaking new ground with development and growth.

As the world recovers from the pandemic, there will be no shortage of challenges in the foreseeable future. It is wise to prepare and grow our capability to face expected and unexpected challenges. Flipping fear, we see excitement. The exciting prospect of tackling a challenge can be created in the workplace and even in our larger ecosystem.

A key difference with a team of innovators is their ability to challenge the status quo with a shared purpose despite differing perspectives and understanding.

There are several steps to fostering constructive expression in the team:

- ➜ start with the purpose and common values of the organisation
- ➜ create psychological safety and support with mutually agreed ground rules
- ➜ share with recognition
- ➜ communicate relevant information for a specific topic
- ➜ establish a process to fairly and transparently capture the expressions
- ➜ keep the discussion in scope
- ➜ embrace the Voice of the Employee as part of the decision-making process.

A resourceful team saves the game

Technology and team working together

Now and then, we all need a helping hand to get stuff done. I cannot imagine being in lockdown without our beloved dishwasher. The machines at home have freed up my time to do other things.

Likewise, businesses have used machinery and automation to improve productivity and product outcomes. Automating manufacturing processes is an ongoing evolution based on market needs and technological advancement.

Car manufacturers are a standout example. Ford started with innovative moving assembly lines back in 1913. Constant improvement of mechanical automation in the 1980s led to digital production systems in the 1990s, and more recently, the adoption of a human and machine collaborative robot (co-bot) in 2016 (The Ford Motor Company, 2019).

Changes can be both exciting and daunting. Change in manufacturing technology can be an exciting new direction for some and brings discomfort for others. The discomfort is because of a general perception that automation and new technologies such as AI and robots will replace humans and take away jobs.

If we look at the workforce in manufacturing over the decades, manual processing jobs have changed over time but have not diminished. A level of mechanical automation has supported manufacturing processes since the industrial revolution. But even with advanced robotic automation, we need responsive teams to manage and work with the automation.

What has changed is that technology has become more advanced, and connecting hardware and software can provide even more intelligent support to a production line and management team. Think of lifting and pouring a large, heavy batch of baking batter every hour in an artisan bakery and the benefit of having a machine that helps.

Automation is more than leveraging machinery to reduce hard physical labour. With digital software, mechanical hardware, and sensors, the combined technologies support humans in more intelligent tasks, such as process flow design with simulation, smart monitoring of production schedule, and responding to potential hazards. The advancement of technology is again supporting the human workforce in some frustrating, repetitive, sometimes hazardous tasks, and we are doing a better job together.

Develop an active thinking culture

Ensuring that products are identical to the design is critical for manufacturing businesses. The level of design and customer needs are built into the product from the start, so changing any details could severely impact how the product performs. Therefore quality control of the outcome is rigid to reduce the possibility of defective products. There are various ways to control product quality, such as implementing statistical measures or inspectors to ensure that the production process meets the specifications. Free-style change decisions without alignment with the needs and requirements add variation to the batch of products. This production method relies heavily on machinery or people willing to comply with the process.

As our economy evolves into customised manufacturing and personalised logistic services, a workforce of active thinkers is crucial to business success. When the needs of the customers and the situations change with minimal notice, the team needs to base their response on the service quality requirements to keep customers satisfied.

Transitioning from following instructions to thinking on their feet can be a steep learning curve for many, particularly when the team first steps into a leadership role with an overwhelming level of responsibility and new problems to solve each day.

Hence it is essential to grow the team by distributing ownership of daily decision-making responsibilities and strengthening communication skills in all business areas.

Ownership and decision-making responsibility can start with micro-delegation until the team and management are comfortable with the increasing delegation of authority. The deliberate decision requires a strong sponsor to support the work programme. Developing the team from operating in the autopilot mode with orders and instructions to being autonomous problem-solving agents across the business will lead to a more active thinking culture. It is an ongoing programme that will help the business shift the dial in adapting to a changing environment with resilience.

Thrive with mojo

'And every day, the world will drag you by the hand, yelling, "This is important! And this is important! And this is important! You need to worry about this! And this! And this!" And each day, it's up to you to yank your hand back, put it on your heart and say, "No. This is what's important."'

– Iain Thomas

In 2020, 75 per cent of employees in the United States and almost 30 per cent of participants in surveys reported symptoms of burnout (de Smet et al., 2021). Pandemic fatigue is caused by the sudden pressure to respond and perform during a crisis, operating instantly in a different business model. The ongoing exhaustion can have a long-lasting effect on the wellness of an organisation and the people. Leaders must find ways to help themselves and the team to thrive with more mojo.

Dare I say, most of the manufacturing and logistics sector suffered from firefighting and fatigue long before the pandemic. That is why better role boundaries, decision-making and adaptivity in a changing environment with a thinking culture is so important in changing the status quo.

However, building capability and skills with an aligned purpose is only part of the solution to re-energise an organisation that is probably operating close to exhaustion after more than two years of reactive management.

Too often, we simply push to do more – and that includes building capability. The reality is that relaxation is more regenerative and can help the team re-energise better and faster than any other method.

Relaxation can come in many forms. Mindfulness and meditation are known to positively impact well-being, and there is plenty of online teaching available. I have found that the practice of meditation can be a big ask for some people, particularly those who can never sit still. It may be why those people are attracted to the industry and entered the manufacturing and the logistics sector in the first place.

Social connection through conversations is another path to relaxation. The conversation needs careful facilitation to provide a supportive environment that makes it safe for participants to share their personal experiences. Facilitators must be trained in active and deep listening skills with empathy. To do this in-house, the facilitators need to ensure they are in a good state of wellness and understand how to safeguard their wellbeing before leading the conversations. Sessions to share the collective experiences and emotions increase personal understanding and create bonding and trust as a team. Insights from the sessions will help understand the team's needs at the psychological level and can be used to change the work conditions to support the team in challenging times.

Relaxation through activities is a practical way for some, whether exercise or recreational hobbies. Playing a sport can clear our minds from daily worries as we focus on hitting the ball or cruising the road on a bike. A freely chosen activity that nourishes our souls can bring more benefits to wellbeing than burning calories.

Quality sleep and sufficient rest directly impact our mojo, although having enough sleep has often been seen as a luxury by many in recent decades as we juggle work, family and personal priorities. Better sleep is essential for the well-being of mind and body. During sleep, our brains form and maintain neural pathways to digest the learning from the day and create new memories. Poor quality sleep or sleep deprivation negatively impacts our body, increasing our chances of high blood pressure, diabetes and cardiovascular diseases (National Institute of Neurological Disorders and Stroke, 2019).

Studies show that sleep deprivation can negatively impact our ability to problem-solve, learn and control our emotions and behaviours. For people who work rotating shifts, variable hours of work affect their body clock and, therefore, their sleep quality. It needs to be counterbalanced with a quiet integration or reflection time, doing activities to calm the mind. Prepare a restful sleeping environment, with light-blocking curtains, cooler air and potential white noise as aids to support better sleep (National Heart Lung and Blood Institute, 2021).

People are the backbone of the success of an organisation. Arianna Huffington, the founder of the Huffington Post, suffered burnout firsthand. She described how the Western workplace culture is 'Single-mindedly obsessed with quarterly earnings reports, maximising short-term profits' (Huffington, 2014).

Logistics and manufacturing businesses suffer from the physical and emotional drain of operating with thin margins. Proactively recognising and injecting much-needed support to reduce stress will have a positive impact. People's health improves with rest and relaxation, bringing better decision-making, more adaptivity, talent retention and productivity. This results in a healthier bottom line and a thriving workplace culture.

PART FOUR

THE VOICE OF PROCESS

Thriving in business requires a coordinated effort. One of the most overlooked elements in improving business performance is the Voice of Process. The enterprise process includes strategic planning, operational activities, data measurements, and performance metrics. Embedding lean and agility in the framework enables the business to change fast in a coordinated fashion. Such an adaptive enterprise process framework is a competitive advantage in challenging times.

The manufacturing and logistics industry has evolved with new technologies coming into play. From the introduction of electricity in the First Industrial Revolution, new materials and standardisation in the Second, and computerisation in the Third, we are in the Fourth with digital technologies, and the Fifth is now emerging.

Industry 4.0 started in 2011 and focuses on smart technologies to perform automation and data to drive intelligent actions (Callaghan Innovation, 2021). Joint cyber-and-physical robotic systems, the IoT, AI, and cloud computing are key technologies being incorporated into the workflow of manufacturing and logistics businesses to improve the efficiency and accuracy of services (Marr, 2018). These technologies are widely used in Intelligent Transport System development around the globe to digitalise transport operation processes to achieve safety, environmental and efficiency outcomes (United Nations Economic Commission for Europe, 2021).

PwC's 2020 Global Digital IQ report revealed that the 5 per cent of companies that invest in digital technologies enterprise-wide have 17 per cent higher profit margin growth over three years (Oxford Economics, 2021). Mastering the integration of adaptive enterprise process management and the ongoing investment in Industry 4.0 technologies will transform business to thrive in the foreseeable future.

The Fifth Industrial Revolution, which arguably started in 2020, involves cognitive computing working with human intelligence (Sarfraz et al., 2021). It is a time when the human mind combines with machine intelligence for more radical innovation in personalising products and services for the masses (Sondh, 2021).

Technologies and minds working together can lead us toward an exponential problem-solving ability and potentially achieving a state of 'neuroenlightment', as Dr John Vervaeke of Toronto University calls it (Vervaeke, 2013). For example, the ability of the human mind to spontaneously resolve the Nine Dots problem was statistically zero, but with the support of neurotechnologies, the statistics of the same experiment rose to 40 per cent.

Technology and human minds joining forces in the field of cognitive science can potentially significantly impact our ability to solve problems that were not accessible in the past, such as climate and environmental issues that threaten society. Projecting the population behaviours in digital twin cities is still a significant challenge because of the complexities of human nature, how we interact with the infrastructure and the nature of the changing environment, including the climate. Greater problem-solving power will potentially help us deal with some of the most critical issues in our supply chain, intelligent transport and logistics systems. These are current developments that present as disruption or opportunity to the sector.

With a glimpse into technological advancement, it is crucial to start building a level of process maturity in the business to prepare for the potential exponential changes.

Enterprise processes and frameworks

Online maps with GPS navigation are a regular feature these days, providing a view of where we start and the way to our destination, as well as finer details of streets and directions. Enterprise processes provide similar clarity about a business's current status and future activities. Traditionally, the enterprise process framework is shown as a visual blueprint of the organisation with the structure of the functions and activities. The visual remains static until it is manually updated. Various teams can glance at it to understand the activities, who is responsible, when they will be triggered, and how the transformation happens to deliver the end service.

A visual enterprise process framework is a handy communication tool to showcase complex groups of activities from a helicopter view. It can have six levels of details, from the highest level (the purpose of the enterprise's existence) down to the sixth level (specific elements of an operational activity) (APQC, 2019).

A sixth level detail is the accounts receivable process that identifies the relevant parties, the payments received channels and any documents needed to complete the transaction. Further 'how to' details are defined in standard operating procedures as an instruction rather than a process document.

With the support of web technology, enterprise processes and different levels of detail can be stored online as living and breathing documentation. They show how business activities are aligned with the organisational purpose and create commercial value for the end customers.

Many businesses have lost the Voice of Process, as anyone and no one owns enterprise processes. The finance team cares about the process of income and expenses, human resources cares about people, performance, and cost of labour, and service delivery cares about customers and revenue. They can have different purposes under an umbrella as an enterprise and their way of doing things. Without the enterprise processes, functions operate in an ad hoc fashion.

Imagine opening the online map again, and this time you see not one but many routes to your destination. The app navigation tells you to stop, start, and take a random way to get from A to B. How uncomfortable does that make your journey? There will be plenty of confusion for the driver and the passengers; it will take far longer than necessary, and you'll spend more on fuel.

Things work better when they are well-designed with users in mind. Human-centric process design cares about people's preferences while clearly laying out the process and actions. We must ensure the key functions and activities are clearly and flexibly connected to save the team from guesswork and rework.

Design for efficiency and differentiation

To design is to conceive and plan with intent. We design devices for a specific function and execute them according to a plan. These short definitions perfectly describe the construction of an enterprise process framework.

Different organisational structures lead to various governance and management roles and the distribution of decision-making power. The last chapter touched on organisational structures such as the traditional hierarchical champagne tower and the more adaptive lean and agile tribe network of origami.

Organisations don't stay the same, and change decisions have a flow-on impact on end-to-end activities at all levels. A Chinese saying is painfully suitable when describing organisational change. It says, 'Pulling a single thread of hair of a person, the rest of the body follows'. Many executives underestimate the consequences of changing a single business area, believing that changes can work in isolation. Experience suggests that it is wiser to review processes and activities with a design hat on to avoid unforeseen consequences that impact business performance in times of change.

One way to identify any flow-on effect is to map out current end-to-end processes. These are called status quo or 'as is' processes. There are different ways to map these.

The top-down design approach uses strategy and enterprise functions as a starting point, identifies the commercial activities, and integrates activities within the systems to hold the team accountable for their actions. The responsibility for designing the integration of the end-to-end activity flow across the functions sits with the organisational change project team with limited input from the line operation team.

Using a co-design approach, it is also possible to build the enterprise process framework from the bottom up. This involves the strategy and the team together deciding what the enterprise process looks like and determining the future process. When change happens, such as team function or technologies, the process can be updated, and teams are given the responsibility to ensure the integration of before and after processes.

The challenge with the bottom-up method is that teams have different perceptions and biases, because activities vary despite standardising the process. People may share contrasting memories and versions of the business activities, creating confusion and excessive work to identify, investigate, and paint an accurate picture of what is going on in the business. This is a common symptom in large corporations with a rich history of change. It is partly why enterprise processes are likely to be designed with top-down decision-making based on a high level of functions and activities.

Without an enterprise process framework, there are likely to be disjointed services to customers, recurring operational problems and decisions to allocate organisational resources based on guesswork which severely impacts the bottom-line revenue.

Clarity with process mapping

Disruption brings the opportunity to create with fewer restrictions. An idea for a new way of doing business needs to be solidified with commercial activities. To be innovative in mapping the business activities requires a clean headspace and an empty drawing space.

The term 'clean headspace' refers to clearing out past and present biases and preconceptions. It is fine to understand the status quo, but it should not define the creation of the future. The empty drawing space policy applies to both existing businesses and new start-ups. A canvas filled with current activities leaves no room for future possibilities to emerge.

Starting with the business purpose and strategy, the renewal of the vision or mission statement is the highest level of the process map. Regardless of the approach, there should be a clear vision of the end goal.

With the vision comes the functions of the business. Despite differences across industry and sector, the core business functions are the input of knowledge, services and materials, processing and selling, or servicing to customers. All other activities support these.

For a business that is entirely internet-based and operates virtually, managing the technology is a core function, and the technology itself is a critical infrastructure across all processes.

The business functions can be separated into departments, with sales and marketing, production or service operation, customer services, financial resources, human resources, assets and technologies management for the traditional businesses. In start-ups, the departmental boundaries blur, with multiple functions resting in a single department. Some activities may be automated with technologies or outsourced to other service providers to focus on core activities.

By now, the new business idea should be confirmed for the creator to see the strategy translated into a flow of commercial value.

The finer details of the business activities can be formulated through iterations. This is when the greater level of details emerges through iteration across the different functions. Implement a co-design process with prospective customers to create a service or products design flow and reduce excessive trial and error. Process co-design can be used to research and develop products, finalise the communication and marketing strategy, and decide the channels for going to market. The exercise ensures that the business activities consistently meet the customers' needs.

The challenge of being too large

Being part of an international enterprise can be exceptionally challenging for process management. No city is the same, yet company headquarters need to standardise their ways of working to maximise efficiency and achieve consistency of services. The culture, working environment, and availability of standardised equipment vary from place to place.

The merger and acquisition history of the enterprise adds to the complexity, with multiple ownership, people, systems, and assets. It would be easy if a change of name and a fresh coat of paint gave people a new sense of identity and the ability to work differently, but changing how things are done is often far more complex.

Managing multiple systems across different time zones and locations can be painful and costly. Understandably, headquarters will want to standardise and streamline systems and processes. The features and functionalities of international systems can be quite different from the local team. While the research and scale of benefit may be justifiable to the highest decision-makers, it is not always cost-effective for local subsidiaries. On one hand, there is a need to obtain transparency with technologies and data internationally. At the same time, local teams have always enjoyed a sense of freedom in working without being closely monitored.

Different needs and perspectives can widen the gap between the local team and the headquarters. Distance and multiple locations mean that managing a change of perspective is limited to short sting visits or even virtual discussions. It takes deliberate leadership to bring teams together with mutual understanding and demonstrate the shared benefits of the changes.

With the disruption of travel and barriers to entry in many countries, internet technologies work well to bring people together. Virtual face-to-face meetings and calls can often bring people closer than in-person meetings. With teams working in the comfort of their own homes and equal front space on the screen, it can encourage some team members to feel more comfortable sharing their voices in virtual meetings.

Making progress with process

Vision leads to strategy, with goals and expectations of results. Between the vision and the outcomes, we need to articulate the strategy into activities and actions. Executives have turned over many stones to find ways to improve performance radically.

There has been a strong emphasis on leadership and culture in the corporate world. I advocate for a healthy organisational culture but am sceptical about people culture as the only thing that drives business improvement. Endless rounds of organisational changes are leaving people with chronic change fatigue. With high-performance culture comes toxic positivity and grinding people down in a high-pressure corporate environment. Clearly, something is not being done right. Leadership and culture change are only part of the solution.

> Technology has become a popular magic bullet.

Everyone is unique, even when similar in personality. Too often, we box people into groups, using assumptions and labels to solve productivity issues. But people are only one factor that impacts whether you and your team are making progress at work.

Technology has become a popular magic bullet. Teams are adding a dash of digital transformation craze on top of the high-performance team cocktail. But any expectations of a quick fix by simply putting technologies in without the support structure further intensify employee burnout.

There is one stone that may have been left unturned. It's how things are done in the business.

There are many ways to conduct business activities, but only one works for you and your organisation. Every business is a unique combination of individuals with their collective experience, history and systems. There is no quick fix or simple equation for getting things done. However, by taking the pressure off the people and implementing process management along with a refreshed culture, you can build your own recipe for success.

Know what you can control

So many things affect business performance. At the micro-level, there is office stationery, the site layout, the equipment,

> Not enough attention is given to controlling the controllables.

the work schedule, and more. The climate, the city transport network and the sector employment market are at the macro-level. While we know these factors can impact the business environment, not enough attention is given to controlling the controllables.

Of course, some factors are unforeseeable. The Global Financial Crisis and natural disasters are outside anyone's control. But the impact of sudden disruption can still be managed through proactive business continuity planning and ensuring there are force majeure clauses in contracts.

The controllable factors are activities with foreseeable likelihoods of risk or success that can be planned and navigated by the management team. Examples are employee safety, production schedules, and staffing.

Controlling the controllable can provide much-needed confidence to the team and stakeholders. Businesses can embrace trial and error in a rapidly changing environment, but resources are scarce, and faith and trust will run out. It is important to set an intention of success and build things to last before jumping onto yet another cycle of testing and mistakes.

Understand process design

A kitchen blender does not function unless parts are in the right place. This concept of Poka-Yoke, the mistake-proofing logic of mechanics, is process design work to prevent unnecessary variation of action and protect the safety of the users.

A mistake-proofing process design does not happen overnight; it is achieved through experimentation, observation and experience over time. To prevent a small child from accidentally turning on a blender, we would have to assume quite different behaviours towards the parts, the buttons and the blades.

Process designed experimentation involves changing a small part of the overall process activities in a controlled environment. That enables us to identify possible risky actions and develop an effective method to limit the variation. Drawing a process diagram can bring the team on board with conceptual thinking and communicate possible consequences of variations. The team needs to document the factors and create hypotheses along with the diagram. There is flexibility to test out various assumptions and theories within the activity.

It is essential to make one small change at a time within the boundaries of the controlled environment, to be clear about what works and what doesn't. We observe the process and the quantifiable results through each experiment, which leads to understanding the best course of action.

In the case of the blender, turning on the power without the parts in perfect alignment can cause the machine to break down and harm people. The next step is to design a mechanism to reduce the possibility of misuse. Some ideas that don't work would break the testing equipment, but that is fine in a controlled environment. The experiment of ideas continues until the best one emerges.

End-to-end process design works on a much larger scale. For example, the blending process is a key activity within a smoothie wholesaler's operation. With a larger scale operation, the risk and setup are entirely different to a small home appliance.

The business process cycle starts with sales and ends with customer services.

Figure 13: Catering and manufacturing process cycle

The end-to-end process can be reviewed using value chain analysis to identify activities that may contribute to greater risk in the overall performance. The experiment will need to be designed with the stakeholders to deliver the expected results.

Ultimately, no executive wants to be surprised by a sudden phone call notifying an accident at work or involving its customer. Yet too often, random probability is left in charge at work without the team even realising it. That is because the end-to-end process was never considered and reviewed with all the risk factors. Understanding process design and how to control the controllable can help prevent unintentional harmful actions to people and the business. Good process design provides confidence in the work outcome and peace of mind for everyone involved.

Line up the resources

Designing the process is half of the business success; the other is planning and execution. Once the experiments are complete, there is an emerging recipe for success in a controlled environment. Scientists have long used this process to solidify discoveries and put the new understanding into practical usage. More than 2000 years ago, Greek mathematician Archimedes, famous for his Eureka moment, realised that his body weight displaced water during a bath. The discovery led to experiments to test the displaced water volume of gold, silver and other objects in a controlled environment. The experiments solved the issue of identifying the impurity of the amount of gold in a crown and led to new understanding of why an object floats on water. It became what we now know as the Archimedes Principle (Bellarmine University, n.d.).

When it comes to putting an idea into production, business-as-usual activities need to run smoothly while the trial takes place. This means clearly defining the trial scope with a specific goal within normal operations.

There are usually multiple process streams in progress when moving goods around in a logistical operation. Similarly, manufacturing production can have concurrent production processes on the shop floor.

The trial may involve a minor alteration to the current operation, such as simply changing the workbench layout. An example might be implementing machinery to help staff in the production department lift heavy loads onto workstations.

The scope of the trial does not require significant additional change support.

A larger trial is like migrating the delivery team from motorbikes to e-scooters. There must be a specific and agreed scope of start and stop points within the overall end-to-end process. Trialling these activities requires additional people resources such as training, change support, potential overtime for the delivery team, and analytical resources to gather data and understand the performance impact.

The key difference is that a small, localised change with minimal alteration to the way of working can be led by the operation team with some project support. In contrast, a significant change of process, such as different transportation delivery modes, requires shifts in the skills, ongoing habits and personal identities of the delivery team. That understanding should be clear in the business case to ensure the process change has sufficient resources to deliver the results sustainably.

Process maturity

Human maturity means to be fully grown and developed physically and emotionally. Many human abilities develop gradually over time through learning and attempting actions. A child learns to eat by coordinating hands to mouth. Around the age of five, the brain masters language, and by age fifteen, it can problem-solve. Scientists have learned that it can take about twenty-five years for the human brain to fully mature (Brodwin, 2017).

Process maturity is the developed ability to visualise, map, and intentionally coordinate activities with resilience and agility within the business. As with our human ability to complete tasks, process maturity isn't complete when the business is conceived. The ability to bring a large group of people together to create coordinated value in commercial activities is acquired through leadership and learning and development.

The more mature, the greater complexity an individual can navigate in life situations. This is similar to the build-up of process maturity in an individual or an organisation. The good news is that process maturity can be fostered and sped up through intentional exercising of process capability muscles.

Starting with learning and development as an introduction, the team needs a basic understanding of business processes and functions, and how they form the basic value chain. That understanding enables them to see beyond their area of responsibility and into the wider end-to-end process. It builds awareness of the activities involved in their responsibility domain.

Before the exercise, it may feel like simply getting jobs done without realising the level of interconnectivity with other parts of the business. Sending out an order and dealing with customers are individual processes, while production schedule planning involves multiple teams. Process awareness is useful when identifying stakeholders and their responsibilities, the actors in the process, and how activities deliver customer outcomes, both internally and externally.

With awareness and understanding comes the opportunity to develop process ideas. In the beginning, it is easier to identify a process within the home team as there is likely to be management support and guidance through the change. Ideally, the change is supported by a process expert such as a Lean Six Sigma black belt to provide independent review and feedback to the team to ensure success.

The interconnectedness of the business will lead to process improvement opportunities with other functions. The more connectivity a process brings, the more complexity during the design and iteration process. With stronger process management muscle and capability, navigating the situations will grow.

Case study: DeliveryFast

With ongoing frustration with daily labour costs and inaccuracies in the production schedule, the team at DeliveryFast decided to put their process improvement learning to use. The team leader started to review their current activities along with customer feedback.

She noted the key priorities for their internal customers were after-hours contact availability and the production schedule delivery time in relation to production starting time.

After some investigation, the team leader found that external factors such as last-minute changes in transportation arrangements can impact the production schedule. This usually happened after hours when the contact person for the scheduling team was not available.

A change of transportation arrangements found in an email inbox is difficult to incorporate in the production scheduling process because the schedule is done manually, two days before the start of production, using spreadsheets and an internal system.

This led the production team to improvise their schedule on the day, and they gradually became less disciplined about following the official plan.

The team leader had a good understanding of the start-to-finish of production scheduling activities. She identified transportation arrangements as a critical input to ensure the schedule was on-point for the production team. Since the scheduling team only worked office hours, it made sense to outsource the after-hours contact to the transportation team as they are the closest to the action. By working closely with the transportation team, unexpected changes could be entered directly into the scheduling system without changing anything.

The schedule still needed to be adjusted with the updated information. The team leader thought hard about how to ensure the schedule reflected the changes on time for the daily production. With guidance from a process expert, the team leader realised that finalising the schedule two days in advance had opened up too much room for last-minute changes. Internal customers wanted the latest schedule six hours before production started.

The team leader reviewed the scheduling process with technologies available in the system and the staffing arrangements. She realised that with the support of the transportation team inputting the changes, her team could use the information in the internal system to adjust the final schedule. Once it was printed, they would need to adjust staffing arrangements. At the beginning of the trial, the changes were done manually, with some of the team working different hours. A regular daily feedback time was established to understand the effectiveness of the process change.

The trial of changing the production schedule time was a success. While occasionally ad hoc changes with transportation happened two hours before the start of production, most changes that happened forty-eight hours prior were captured. This resulted in a more reliable production schedule and made it easier for the production team to juggle some of the smaller changes. The changes positively impacted the customer satisfaction score and labour costs, and fully enforced the production schedule.

Since then, the team has been looking at innovations to automate the sharing of production schedules through mobile devices with apps rather than having them on the office desktop computer. It will continually update those teams who are always on the move on the schedule and provide further flexibility in smart production scheduling in the future.

Organisation process maturity

How do we gain an understanding of the level of organisational process maturity? The level of organisational process maturity can be assessed through the voice of various parties involved in the business. Financial reports, customer needs, employee feedback, and systems issue logs are included in a process maturity toolbox. Having a good set of tools provides momentum and speed, whether building new or improving the current understanding in process management.

Entering into a digital era, manufacturing and logistics companies have started to adopt technologies into the processes. Hybrid processes with machines, digital or not, working alongside humans is a common sight.

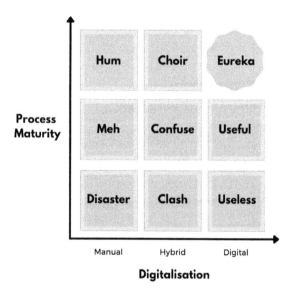

Figure 14: Digital process maturity model

There are three possible outcomes in hybrid process maturity when incorporating digital technologies.

Clashing is a common sight in an organisation with relatively low process maturity and team coordination. It seems complicated to get people to do the right things, and there are likely conflicting priorities and constant firefighting due to unplanned changes. Lack of clarity means it is difficult to understand what is going on in the business. Executives at this level have to brace themselves for constant unpleasant surprises and find ways to keep themselves safe in the environment. There is little physical and psychological safety.

Confusion is slightly better than being in clashes or conflicts. The level of firefighting is bearable, although not pleasant. The number of priorities to be juggled are still significant though manageable at the expense of additional resources. There is plenty of confusion about responsibilities, processes, and timing. Some motivated teams will try to fill the gap with their initiatives. However, it is based more on people's knowledge rather than a coordinated, structured way of working. That is frustrating because executives face constantly changing performance when people move and change things around without anyone knowing.

Have you ever been to a choir concert? The harmony of voices across different vocal ranges with the music can be really moving. The best version of organisation process maturity is like a well-rehearsed choir. The singers do well individually, without the need to outshine each other. Together, their performance is a spectacular joint effort.

At the **Choir** level of maturity, an organisation has clarity of purpose, intentional activities, and outcomes. There is consistency in performing coordinated activities across different functions with agility, which is soothing in a busy environment. The ability to exceed expectations leaves a lasting impression on customers. While things can still go wrong, when issues arise, it is clear who is responsible for the process and how everyone can be involved to reduce the impact. Thorough process improvement with the team reduces the possibility of the same problems happening again. As with choir practice, there's a will to create a stellar performance every time. It is a shared team effort that makes the performance memorable.

Whether the organisation adopts hybrid or fully digital processes, the fundamental requirement is a basic level of process maturity to enable connectivity and flow of the enterprise processes to enable people and technologies to perform.

Process performance limits

Process limits are essential to achieving greater organisational process maturity, particularly for those looking to alter processes with quality results. It is part of a statistical method to measure the variations of an activity to know if the process is within the range of upper and lower limits.

One example is the morning commute to work time for an individual. The process starts when Hilary leaves home and stops when she arrives at the office car park. On most days, the drive takes her twenty to thirty minutes. However, looking at her mobile map, she realised that it took longer than an hour over a handful of days over the past month. On one of those days, she spent ninety minutes in the car.

If we translate it into technical terms, the upper limit for the driving to work process is thirty minutes. If all traffic lights were green and there was little traffic, it could take twenty minutes, which is the lower limit of the process performance of this route. Technically speaking, these are the control limits for Hilary's daily commute by the measure of time. Anything outside these control limits is an anomaly or, as we sometimes call it, an 'out of control' point.

Exceptional situations happen, such as when Hilary took ninety minutes to drive to work. This data point is outside of the control limit range. Hilary shared her data with her family, and her mum wondered what had happened. Hilary remembered sitting in gridlock in poor weather, with a broken car blocking lanes on the highway.

Measuring and gathering the data points of the driving process helps us understand how often the driving time took longer than expected. When data points fall outside the upper or lower limit, it is worthwhile to look for any repeated, outside the norm situations. The beauty of having an app is that it provides plenty of information about routes. However, the richness of the data comes from Hilary, who vividly remembered the pain of sitting still in traffic listening to the car radio.

If the exceptions had happened more regularly, Hilary would have decided to drive a different route to the office. That is because, without realising it, she had already gathered enough mental data to know when the highway was busy and to avoid the route. This could be further broken down by measuring the time she entered the on-ramp and got off the highway because her mobile app captures the location and time. A granular level of process limits can be created just for the section along the highway. In that case, process limits change, and a new measure starts when the change happens.

The process limits help us observe and understand the factors and variations in performance. Different people, types of vehicles, the age of the fleet all make a difference to the journey. If we gather the data from a fleet of vehicles, it is possible to view them as individual vehicles or as a whole. Consolidating the fleet comes with a holistic view of the fleet time on the road as a team. Imagine combining various data sources such as the roster of drivers, their skill level, traffic conditions and weather, and the richness of the information from consolidated data can provide significant clarity of the operations and the output.

Why is it important to know about the process performance limits? Because process maturity is mainly dependent on methodological problem solving with facts and data in an organisation.

Think about our earlier conversation about human maturity, which comes with the ability to observe people and surroundings, isolate unrelated events, and obtain useful data to assess the best course of action. There is an element of uncertainty in every situation, but having a level of maturity equips us to navigate the unknown with greater comfort, based on data from our past experiences.

It is no different for an organisation, particularly for larger corporates where there is unlimited raw data from various internal sources and people's experiences are within reach. The collective wisdom of people's knowledge, experience and process data is an untapped resource that has not been fully utilised and leads to missed opportunities. If those were the raw bulk rocks, it would have been a waste to not look into them and find the hidden gemstones within.

Digitalise successfully

Large enterprises have sped up the deployment of infrastructure and operations technologies despite the delay of investment in 2020. There has been a 20 per cent increase since 2019. The acceleration supports the transition to a new working environment, enabling employees to be productive while working remotely due to COVID-19 impacts, and investing with a focus on resilience and future competitiveness in the new digital era.

With that, executives of large enterprises outside the IT space have jumped ahead with investing in monitoring technologies, such as AI and IoT. In 2019, 17 per cent of IT automation technologies on the roadmap were in implementation, which increased to 45 per cent in 2020 (Gartner, Inc, 2020).

At a CIO award ceremony in 2021, Kevin Drinkwater, one of New Zealand's top fifty chief information officers, said, 'If you can't do it manually and explain it, you can't get a computer to automate it'.

Many enterprises still suffer from chasing shiny new things. They forget that they must get the foundation right to get automation right. A good solid digital automation has to start from a well-performed and precise manual process with absolute clarity in the performance measure.

The digital goddess cannot grant ambiguous wishes because the digital world can only cope with black and white at this point. If the process cannot be translated into computer language, it cannot be done. The computer can only cope with precision if you need a particular outcome. It is like planning a road trip. What is the starting point, and where is the destination? How much time do we have to get there? Who else will be in the car? How do we know we are on the right track to where we want to be? Those details must be decided before the method of transport is considered. While many of us have experience planning a road trip, planning technology automation isn't an everyday adventure.

No rule of thumb says the transition from manual to digital must be done in a big blast – although we have seen many corporations have taken that route. A digital transformation programme with too many initiatives that impact the majority of the business functions in a short timeframe is extremely risky. It is no different from building a tall Jenga tower while removing the bottom pieces.

Snakes and ladders of digital change

In my observation, many digital change decisions have been like a game of Snakes and Ladders, where a throw of the dice can either take you ahead or move you back. While there aren't any dice in the journey of digital change, migrating successfully from manual to digital requires understanding, good judgment, and informed decisions along the way. Without these, the success of digital changes is a matter of luck.

Each player in the digital journey has a different starting point and plays alone. How do you know where the starting point is? Understanding the maturity of the organisational process will help determine it. Is there consistency in the way of working and the output? What's the difference between branches and countries? Can the customer distinguish the quality of different products?

The next thing is to assess the level of digital technology in use and how well it delivers the ideal functionalities and supports business processes. What is already in place to help people get work done? Are the technologies producing a desired or intended result? Do the assessment in-house with a set of questionnaires or with external benchmarking and industry standards.

Not every organisation should digitise their entire business. If a unique value proposition of manual creative process is involved, consider digital technologies as supporting functions, such as sales distribution channels, rather than the primary production.

Once the starting point is determined, decide on the most practical steps and which technologies are the best fit. Note that the journey of digital change is single-player only. There is no reason to compare your pace of technological change with others because everyone has a different starting point.

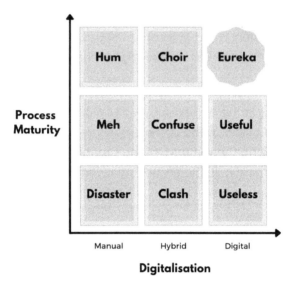

Figure 15: Digital process maturity model

The model in figure 15 describes the relationship between process maturity and the success of transforming the business operations, with various degrees of digital systems support. Greater process maturity in the organisation increases the likelihood of achieving strategic success when using digital technologies to deliver innovation and create exceptional value-added customer experiences.

The relationship of process and digital change

Understanding how the organisation gets work done is crucial to digital success. Is it heavily reliant on people doing things manually? If so, is the performance of that work poor, good, or excellent? How do we define good and excellent performance? What measures do we have? Those questions start your understanding of the organisation process maturity and provide insight into the readiness for automation. Repeat these questions for specific functional departments and the more granular operational process before committing to an automation project.

If the maturity of the manual process is poor, digitising the process can turn into a disaster with a lack of clarity and flipping decisions about what the outcomes should be. However, some executives might find it challenging to commit to more groundwork before acquiring new technologies. A short-term view of success leads to a failed investment in digital transformation and rework for many years to come.

Adding technologies into an already messy manual processing environment will only cause more clashes. In such a hybrid environment, the manual processes do not perform to the required level, and added technologies cause more clashes – further reducing productivity. That is when decision-makers often jump the gun to implement technologies such as automation without clarity or careful planning in the people and technologies interaction.

Some might decide that the manual processes are not working well, and it is easier to digitalise and automate the work fully. Without process maturity, the outcome is completely useless and does not perform. That is no different to throwing money in the ocean.

Into the future

Organisations that fall into the hype of technology trends and lose their soul will not win customers' hearts. The organisation's purpose should be at the core of decision-making about changes to organisational processes and technologies. Digital technologies are quickly becoming commodities instead of a point of difference. Holding on to the most valuable proposition while meeting market needs using technologies is crucial for businesses to remain competitive in a changing and disrupted marketplace.

The ability to understand and retain the unique value proposition lies in understanding the Voice of the Organisation. It is the unified voice of the business, the customers, the employees and the process. This cohesive voice and the combined power provide radical clarity and empowered strategic decisions for the organisation to thrive.

An empowered future can look different for every organisation. Some thrive with manual process excellence with minimal digital technologies. Their decision-making is strong through a network of close-knit relationships and communication with the team. The organisation is constantly evolving with agility and resilience to changing market needs. Some say an environment where manual processes work perfectly sounds like a soothing hum.

For many, the ideal is having digital technologies and people complement each other in the organisation work process. A hybrid environment created with software and hardware relieves people from repetitive processes, and data insights lead to opportunities for greater efficiency and creativity. The outcome is like a single person singing and recording videos at different ranges, using technologies to form a one-person choir. A well-designed digital and human strategy brings clarity and new possibilities for the organisation.

It is arguable whether any logistics and manufacturing company can completely digitalise the entire business, moving away from owning or leasing physical assets such as building and fleet of transport. In this case, the ideal stage of completely digitising the organisation is the power of integrated data in real-time. This brings breakthroughs in the speed of understanding the Voice of the Organisation. The clarity of data insights helps improve efficiency and uncover commercial opportunities.

An organisation with a clear voice from the power of connected, real-time data is more likely to have a eureka moment tapping into a new uncontested market, solving new problems and creating new demand in the market space.

Afterword

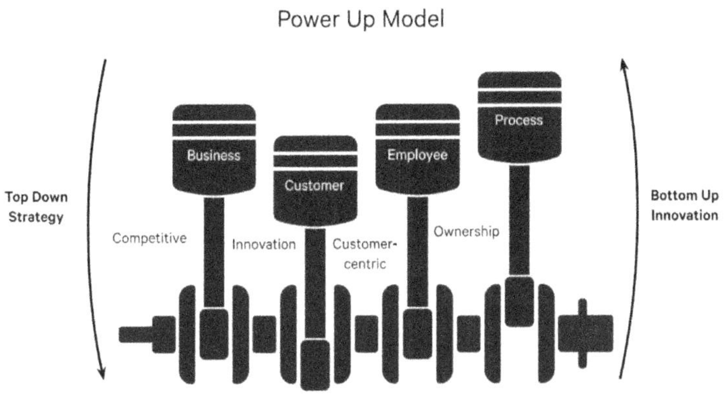

Power Up Model

Figure 16: Power Up model

Seek radical clarity

Business leaders need to be challengers who can integrate the business needs and innovate by breaking down historical systemic barriers with the support of technologies.

Radical clarity is at the heart of this model to ignite the power to lift capability and improve alignment across the business to thrive in the future.

We know that technologies will play an increasingly important role in the sector, enabling more productivity and creating new opportunities from innovation. As the metaverse of digital technology becomes the new normal, our physical living will be more integrated with virtual reality, and different lifestyles will emerge. It will likely further disrupt the way

202 | POWER UP

people, including our teams, interact with each other and the customers' expectations of service and products.

While no single action plan will work for all when navigating toward a brighter, commercially sustainable business future in a changing environment, getting closer to a clear focal point by connecting with the voices and process data within the organisation will help.

Executive leadership's responsibility is to show the team a clear path ahead. With the changes, it is crucial to have clarity of the organisation's unique value proposition and the collective wisdom gathered through its history. Throughout the book, I have shared pragmatic practices so that leaders can power up their productivity, innovations, and future careers in leading organisational changes. The heavy lifting can be made easier by empowering teams to share the responsibility, encouraging them to innovate and move toward digital agility across the organisation.

Call to action

It is time to equip courageous leaders to step up and lead the way forward with clarity – particularly across an industry hammered by changing global logistics needs, a disrupted supply chain and emerging transportation technologies.

To be an effective leader of tomorrow's world, leaders need to learn new skills to engage their teams in the new hybrid environment. They must harness practical, data-driven problem-solving skills and increase their capacity to lead and implement sustainable solutions with technology.

CHRISTINE W.K. YIP

If you'd like to know more, get in touch to discuss online or in-person training customised to your unique team situation.

Or if you'd like a conversation about how to move forward in identifying innovation and productivity wins to lift performance with an in-house session, online or in-person, let's talk.

About the Author

Christine Yip is a ferocious advocate for clarity in business processes. As an independent business improvement advisor, she specialises in digital systems, enterprise processes, and project management.

She has fifteen years of experience leading and implementing technology and business processes across manufacturing, logistics, government and aviation. In 2020, Christine won the New Zealand Top 50 CIO award for a programme of work delivered internally and externally with airline clients.

Known by colleagues and friends for her radically fresh, disruptive perspective and thinking, Christine has a pragmatic approach to getting things done. She works with leaders and teams in infrastructure-heavy manufacturing and logistics businesses ambitious to grow through innovation.

Christine's other passion is psychology, and her reading list ranges from Confucius to Carl Jung. She lives in Auckland, New Zealand, with her partner (and fellow advocate of Open Source technologies), Glen. They share a chocolate point Siamese cat, a prolific vegetable garden, and chickens that keep them well-supplied with eggs.

You can contact Christine via email at christine@cwhy.co.nz

On LinkedIn https://www.linkedin.com/in/christinewky/

Or go to her website: www.cwhy.co.nz

For resources related to this book, visit: cwhy.co.nz/book

References

The Voice of Business

Alicke, K., & Lösch, M. (2010, January 1). *Lean and Mean: How does your supply chain shape up?* McKinsey. https://www.mckinsey.com/~/media/mckinsey/dotcom/client_service/operations/pdfs/lean_and_mean-how_does_your_supply_chain_shape_up.pdf.

Bucy, M., Finlayson, A., Kelly, G., & Moye, C. (2020, November 18). *The 'How' of Transformation.* McKinsey & Company. https://www.mckinsey.com/industries/retail/our-insights/the-how-of-transformation.

Cleary, S. (Ed), (2004). *Communication: A Hands-on Approach.* Juta: Lansdowne.

Cowen, T. (2021, October 12). *There Is No Shortage of Reasons for the Broken Supply Chain.* Bloomberg. https://www.bloomberg.com/opinion/articles/2021-10-11/supply-chain-disruptions-almost-too-many-reasons-to-count.

Koetsier, J. (2020, September 10). *97 per cent of Executives Say Covid-19 Sped Up Digital Transformation.* Forbes. https://www.forbes.com/sites/johnkoetsier/2020/09/10/97-of-executives-say-covid-19-sped-up-digital-transformation/?sh=52c29fb74799.

Kubiak, T.M., & Benbow, D. W. (2007). *The Certified Six Sigma Black Belt Handbook.* Milwaukee: ASQ Quality Press.

Lencioni, P. (2006). *Silos, Politics and Turf Wars: A Leadership Fable About Destroying the Barriers That Turn Colleagues Into Competitors* (1st ed.). San Francisco: Jossey-Bass.

McKinsey & Company. (2019, July 12). *Why do most transformations fail? A conversation with Harry Robinson*. McKinsey. https://www.mckinsey.com/business-functions/transformation/our-insights/why-do-most-transformations-fail-a-conversation-with-harry-robinson

Mckinsey & Company. (2020, October 5). *How COVID-19 has pushed companies over the technology tipping point—and transformed business forever*. McKinsey. https://www.mckinsey.com/business-functions/strategy-and-corporate-finance/our-insights/how-covid-19-has-pushed-companies-over-the-technology-tipping-point-and-transformed-business-forever.

Mitchell, J. S. (2002, January 1). *Best Practices Maintenance Benchmarks*. Maintenance Benchmarking. http://www.maintenancebenchmarking.com/best_practice_maintenance.htm

Miller, J. G., & Vollmann, T. E. (1985, September 1). *The Hidden Factory*. Harvard Business Review. https://hbr.org/1985/09/the-hidden-factory

Quast, L. (2012, August 20). *Why Knowledge Management Is Important To The Success Of Your Company*. Forbes. https://www.forbes.com/sites/lisaquast/2012/08/20/why-knowledge-management-is-important-to-the-success-of-your-company/?sh=59080eae3681.

Schafer, S. (2021, April 13). *Metrics & Benchmarking for Manufacturing Companies*. Smith Schafer Associates, Ltd. https://blog.smithschafer.com/metrics-benchmarking-for-manufacturing-companies.

Sye, G. L. (2009). *Process Mastery with Lean Six Sigma* (2nd ed.). Queensland: Soarent Publication.

The Voice of the Customer

Elkington, J. (2018, June 25). *25 Years Ago I Coined the Phrase "Triple Bottom Line." Here's Why It's Time to Rethink It.* Harvard Business Review. https://hbr.org/2018/06/25-years-ago-i-coined-the-phrase-triple-bottom-line-heres-why-im-giving-up-on-it

Haller, K., Lee, J., & Cheung, J. (2020, June). *2020 Consumers driving change*. IBM Corporation. https://www.ibm.com/thought-leadership/institute-business-value/report/consumer-2020.

International Monetary Fund. (2021, October 15). *Regional Economic Outlook for Asia and Pacific, October 2021*. IMF. https://www.imf.org/en/Publications/REO/APAC/Issues/2021/10/15/regional-economic-outlook-for-asia-and-pacific-october-2021

Kubiak, T.M., & Benbow, D.W. (2016). *The Certified Six Sigma Black Belt Handbook, Third Edition*. Milwaukee: ASQ Quality Press.

Medelyan, A. (2021, July 5). *How to theme qualitative data using AI analysis software*. Insights Thematic. https://

getthematic.com/insights/theme-qualitative-data-using-ai/

PricewaterhouseCoopers. (2021, June). *PwC's Global Consumer Insights Survey 2021*. PwC. https://www.pwc.com/gx/en/consumer-markets/consumer-insights-survey/2021/gcis-june-2021.pdf

Mt Ommaney, Qld.Thematic. (2018, November 15). *See why Greyhound love using Thematic for their customer feedback analysis*. Thematic. https://www.youtube.com/watch?v=_ZMy6kpxxO4&t=2s

Wargo, E. (2016, July 1). *How Many Seconds to a First Impression?* Association of Psychological Science. https://www.psychologicalscience.org/observer/how-many-seconds-to-a-first-impression.

The Voice of the Employee

ATA. (2019, 7 1). *Truck Driver Shortage Report 2019*. ATA. https://www.trucking.org/sites/default/files/2020-01/ATAs%20Driver%20Shortage%20Report%202019%20with%20cover.pdf

De Bono, E. (1985). *Six Thinking Hats*. Toronto: Key Porter Books.

de Smet, A., Tegelberg, L., Theunissen, R., & Vogel, T. (2021, March 1). *Overcoming pandemic fatigue: How to reenergize organizations for the long run*. McKinsey & Company. https://www.mckinsey.com/business-functions/people-and-organizational-performance/

our-insights/overcoming-pandemic-fatigue-how-to-
reenergize-organizations-for-the-long-run

Ellis, A. (2020, January 1). *Anne Ellis*. PeopleMap. http://www.
peoplemaps.com/anne-ellis/

Fry, R. (2020, 4 28). *Millennials overtake Baby Boomers as
America's largest generation*. Pew Research Center.
https://www.pewresearch.org/fact-tank/2020/04/28/
millennials-overtake-baby-boomers-as-americas-largest-
generation/

Huffington, A. (2014). *Thrive*. New York: Penguin Random
House.

IRU. (2021, October 1). *New IRU survey shows driver
shortages to soar in 2021*. International Road and
Transport Union. https://www.iru.org/news-resources/
newsroom/new-iru-survey-shows-driver-shortages-
soar-2021

Kahneman, D. (2013). *Thinking, Fast and Slow*. New York:
Farrar, Straus and Giroux.

Levine, S. R. (2019, February 26). *Outperform With A Growth
Mindset Culture*. Forbes. https://www.forbes.com/sites/
forbesinsights/2019/02/26/outperform-with-a-growth-
mindset-culture/?sh=3ca76ad73c2c

Maslow, A.H. (1943). *A Theory of Human Motivation*.
American Psychological Association. https://www.apa.
org/pubs/journals

Myers, I. (1962). *The Myers Briggs type indicator Manual*. Consulting Psychologists Press. https://psycnet.apa.org/record/2013-29682-000

National Heart Lung and Blood Institute. (2021, June 29). *Sleep Deprivation and Deficiency | NHLBI, NIH*. https://www.nhlbi.nih.gov/health-topics/sleep-deprivation-and-deficiency

National Institute of Neurological Disorders and Stroke. (2019, August 13). *Brain Basics: Understanding Sleep*. https://www.ninds.nih.gov/Disorders/Patient-Caregiver-Education/understanding-Sleep

Noji, T. (2019). *TOYOTA MONOGATARI* (X. Chan, Trans.; First ed.). EcoTrend Publications.

OECD. (2021). *OECD sees brighter economic prospects but an uneven recovery - OECD*. https://www.oecd.org/newsroom/oecd-sees-brighter-economic-prospects-but-an-uneven-recovery.htm

Rouzet, D., Sánchez, A. C., Renault, T., & Roehn, O. (2019, 9 10). *Fiscal challenges and inclusive growth in ageing societies*. OECD. https://www.oecd-ilibrary.org/economics/fiscal-challenges-and-inclusive-growth-in-ageing-societies_c553d8d2-en

Sinek, S. (2011). *Start With Why: How great leaders inspire everyone to take action*. London: Penguin Books Limited.

The Ford Motor Company. (2019, September 26). *Ford Choreographs Robots to Help People – and Each Other – On the Fiesta Assembly Line*. Ford Media Centre.

https://media.ford.com/content/fordmedia/feu/en/
news/2019/09/26/ford-choreographs-robots-to-help-
people--and-each-other--on-the-.html

The World Bank. (2021). *East Asia & Pacific | Data*. Retrieved
16 November 2021, from https://data.worldbank.org/
country/Z4

Toyota Motor Corporation. (2012, 1 1). *The 75-year history
through text*. Toyota Motor Corporation. https://www.
toyota-global.com/company/history_of_toyota/75years/
text/index.html

Virgin Atlantic. (2019, January 1). *Our People*. Virgin Atlantic.
https://corporate.virginatlantic.com/gb/en/sustainability/
programme-overview/people.html#:~:text=Our%20
vision%20is%20to%20be%20the%20most%20loved%20
travel%20company.

Wansink, B., & Sobal, J. (2007, January 1). *So many
decisions, so little time...* Cornell University. https://
evidencebasedliving.human.cornell.edu/2010/03/02/so-
many-decisions-so-little-time/

The Voice of Process

APQC. (2019, September 26). *Process Classification
Framework (PCF)®*. APQC. https://www.apqc.org/
resource-library/resource-listing/apqc-process-
classification-framework-pcf-cross-industry-excel-7

Asian Development Bank. (2021, May 31). *Developing Asia
to Grow 7.3% in 2021 Even as COVID-19 Lingers*. https://

www.adb.org/news/developing-asia-grow-7-3-2021-even-covid-19-lingers

Bellarmine University. (n.d.). *About Eureka!* https://www.bellarmine.edu/learningcommunity/eureka/about/

Brodwin, E. S. G. (2017, November 7). *Here are the ages your brain matures at everything.* Business Insider Australia. https://www.businessinsider.com.au/age-brain-matures-at-everything-2017-11?r=US&IR=T

Callaghan Innovation. (2021, August 1). *Industry 4.0 Hub The fourth industrial revolution has begun. Are you ready?* Technology and product development. https://www.callaghaninnovation.govt.nz/industry-4

Gartner, Inc. (2020, December 1). *2020-2022 Emerging Technology Roadmap for Large Enterprises.* Gartner: Global Research and Advisory Company. https://emtemp.gcom.cloud/ngw/globalassets/en/information-technology/documents/benchmarks/emerging-tech-roadmap-le-2020-2022.pdf

Marr, B. (2018, September 2). *What is Industry 4.0? Here's A Super Easy Explanation For Anyone.* Forbes. https://www.forbes.com/sites/bernardmarr/2018/09/02/what-is-industry-4-0-heres-a-super-easy-explanation-for-anyone/?sh=145eae589788

Oxford Economics. (2021, August 1). *2020 Global Digital IQ. Buckle up. Uncertainty is back.* https://www.pwc.com/us/en/library/digital-iq.html

Sarfraz, Z., Sarfraz, A., Iftikar, H. M., & Akhund, R. (2021, April). *Is COVID-19 pushing us to the Fifth Industrial Revolution (Society 5.0)?* Pakistan Journal of Medical Sciences. https://www.ncbi.nlm.nih.gov/pmc/articles/ PMC7931290/ 37(2), 591–594.

Sondh, K. (2021, April 29). *In the 5th Industrial Revolution, creativity must meet technology.* Oxford Economics. http://blog.oxfordeconomics.com/world-post-covid/ in-the-5th-industrial-revolution-creativity-must-meet-technology

United Nations Economic Commission for Europe. (2021, February 25). *Countries endorse UNECE Roadmap to strengthen harmonization of Intelligent Transport Systems | UNECE.* UNECE. https://unece.org/sustainable-development/press/countries-endorse-unece-roadmap-strengthen-harmonization-intelligent

Vervaeke, J. (2013, July 20). *Neuroenlightenment: John Vervaeke at TEDxUofT.* TEDx University of Toronto. https://www.youtube.com/watch?v=qKvRUfZ_u1o

List of Figures and Tables

www.ingramcontent.com/pod-product-compliance
Lightning Source LLC
Chambersburg PA
CBHW070943050326
40689CB00014B/3328